Iceland

Iceland

By Barbara A. Somervill

Enchantment of the World™
Second Series

Children's Press®

An Imprint of Scholastic Inc.

New York Toronto London Auckland Sydney
Mexico City New Delhi Hong Kong
Danbury, Connecticut

Frontispiece: Hallgrímskirkja in Reykjavík

Consultant: Kirsten Wolf, Department of Scandinavian Studies, University of Wisconsin–Madison

Please note: All statistics are as up-to-date as possible at the time of publication.

Book production by The Design Lab

  Library of Congress Cataloging-in-Publication Data

Somervill, Barbara A.
  Iceland / by Barbara A. Somervill.
      pages cm. — (Enchantment of the world. Second series)
  Includes bibliographical references and index.
  ISBN 978-0-531-25602-2 (lib. bdg. : alkaline paper)
1. Iceland—Juvenile literature. I. Title.

  DL305.S662 2013
  949.12—dc23   2012047117

1 2 3 4 5 6 7 8 9 10 R 22 21 20 19 18 17 16 15 14 13

Iceland

Contents

Cover photo:
Aurora borealis

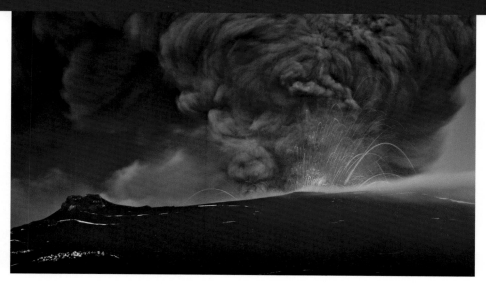

Eyjafjallajökull volcano

Gyrfalcon

A Lifetime on the Sea

THE ALARM GOES OFF, AND EINAR ROLLS OUT OF BED. It is 2:00 a.m., but it is already light out. Akureyri, where Einar lives, is close to the Arctic Circle, and the sun is not down for long during the summer months. Einar pulls on a shirt, sweater, jeans, and a pair of heavy wool socks. His mother calls, and he heads to the kitchen for breakfast.

Einar's father, Magnús, is already at the table. The two enjoy bowls of oatmeal laced with honey and almonds. Einar finishes his oatmeal, opens a pot of *skyr*, a thick yogurt-like soft cheese, and stirs in goji berries and raisins. Skyr is sweet, tart, and delicious!

After breakfast, Einar slides his feet into waterproof boots. He and Magnús head down to the harbor, where the family's fishing vessel is docked. By 3:00 a.m., the crew is aboard and heading out to sea. Although Einar is only fourteen years old, he has been fishing with his father during the summer for several years. This is how the tradition of fishing is passed down from generation to generation in the Icelandic community of Akureyri.

Opposite: **Fishing villages dot the coast of Iceland.**

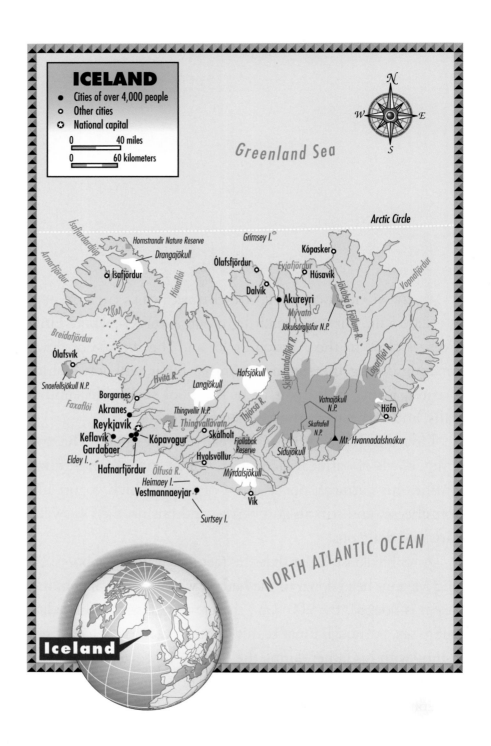

ICELAND

- ● Cities of over 4,000 people
- ○ Other cities
- ✪ National capital

0   40 miles

0   60 kilometers

Greenland Sea

N
W E
S

Arctic Circle

Ísafjardardjúp

Hornstrandir Nature Reserve

Drangajökull

Grímsey I.

Kópasker

Ólafsfjördur

Eyjafjördur

Húsavik

Arnarfjördur

Ísafjördur

Dalvik

Akureyri

Húnaflói

Myvatn

Jökulsá á Fjöllum R.

Jökulsárgljúfur N.P.

Vopnafjördur

Breidafjördur

Skjálfandafljót R.

Lagarfljót R.

Ólafsvik

Hofsjökull

Snaefellsjökull N.P.

Langjökull

Hvitá R.

Borgarnes

Vatnajökull N.P.

Höfn

Akranes

Faxaflói

Thingvellir N.P.

Thjorsá R.

Skaftafell N.P.

Reykjavik

L. Thingvallavatn

Skálholt

Keflavik

Kópavogur

Fjallabak Reserve

Mt. Hvannadalshnúkur

Gardabaer

Sídujökull

Eldey I.

Hyolsvöllur

Hafnarfjördur

Ölfusá R.

Myrdalsjökull

Heimaey I.

Vestmannaeyjar

Vik

Surtsey I.

NORTH ATLANTIC OCEAN

Iceland

Einar's family tree is filled with fishers. His father and uncle fish from the same boat that their father sailed. Now Einar's grandfather is retired. When the family gets together, they all talk fishing.

The crew works tirelessly preparing for the catch. The *Halldór Laxness*, Einar's family ship, is a trawler. The ship drags a large net through the water just below the vessel. Today the crew is fishing for blue whiting. On the journey out to sea, the crew checks the net carefully. The condition of the net is critical. If a net tears during a large haul, the day's catch could

About 4,500 Icelanders make a living by fishing.

be lost. Any tears or weakness in the mesh must be repaired before the net is lowered into the water. This job is neither quick nor easy. The open end of the net can measure as large as five football fields. Because Einar is still learning, he works with his uncle Björn, who has more than twenty years' experience as a fisher. It will be several years before Einar will be allowed to do any repair work without supervision.

It is a lucky day for Einar and his family. The sonar equipment locates a large school of whiting to the northwest. A large haul early in the day means a shorter workday and a good profit. All hands are on deck as the winch lowers the massive net into the sea.

A fisher in Iceland checks his net.

Once the line is overboard, it's time for a morning snack. In the galley, the crew chows down on thick slices of rye bread, cheese, cold sausages, and skyr. There are few meals that do not include skyr, either as a main dish or dessert. Einar is having a growth spurt, and the crew members tease him about the amount of food he eats.

The crew of the *Halldór Laxness* has been together for more than a dozen years. They are bound by their work like a family is bound by blood. Every crew member either is related to Einar or has known him since he was a toddler. In Akureyri, this too is part of the fishing life.

The community's economy depends on fishing and whale watching. Many of the people in the town catch fish, process fish, sell fish, or supply the boats that go fishing. When the catch is good, the community thrives. During years when the catch is poor, the people struggle together.

More than 40 percent of all the fish caught in Iceland are brought in by trawlers.

Today's fishing is a great success. By 11:00 a.m., the *Halldór Laxness* is heading home. Once the fish are hauled on board, the crew settles down to a meal of hot dogs and potato salad. It's Einar's turn to wash the dishes and clean up the galley.

Einar and Magnús arrive back home by 3:00 p.m. Einar's mother has prepared a meal of rich lamb stew, boiled potatoes, beets, and cabbage. Einar yawns and heads upstairs to bed. Though it's only 4:00 in the afternoon, Einar has already put in a long, demanding day's work, and he's tired.

First Name Basis

In much of the world, people have a given name and a family name. The family name is passed on from parent to child. Iceland uses a different system. In Iceland, a person's last name consists of his or her father's first name followed by the Icelandic word for *son* or *daughter*. Einar Magnússon got his last name because his father's name is Magnús. He is Einar, the son of Magnús. Magnússon is a patronymic, which means "father's name." In some cases, Icelanders use the mother's first name to create the child's last name. This is called a matronymic.

In the United States, a person writing or speaking about a man named John Smith might call him "Mr. Smith" or "Smith." In Iceland, people are always called by their first names, even in formal situations. This custom is followed throughout this book.

When summer ends, Einar will return to school for his last year at the compulsory school. After finishing school, he plans to continue fishing with his father on the *Halldór Laxness*. Like his father, Einar is looking forward to a lifetime on the seas.

Icelanders enjoy a hearty meal after a hard day's work.

The Force of Nature

O N May 21, 2011, Iceland's most active volcano erupted. Grímsvötn lies under the Vatnajökull glacier in southeastern Iceland. The eruption began with a series of small earthquakes that shook Iceland's central region. Then smoke rose from the volcano. The plume of ash and steam climbed 12 miles (20 kilometers) high. The ash disrupted air traffic, as the Icelandic government declared a no-fly zone for jets within 138 miles (222 km). When the volcano Eyjafjallajökull erupted in 2010, it created such a massive ash cloud that planes could not fly between North America and Europe for several days.

Volcanic eruptions and earthquakes come as no surprise to Icelanders. Iceland was created as the result of erupting volcanoes. For thousands of years, volcanoes beneath the Atlantic Ocean have oozed lava and formed the foundation of Iceland. Iceland has about two hundred volcanoes, although only thirty-five are considered active.

Opposite: **The eruption of Eyjafjallajökull in 2010 caused more than one hundred thousand flights to be canceled. It was the largest disruption to air traffic since World War II.**

Deadly Eruption

In 1783, cracks opened in the earth on either side of Iceland's Mount Laki. The cracks began oozing lava and clouds of poisonous gas. The eruption continued for more than eight months. More than half of Iceland's livestock died. People starved, and Iceland lost one-fourth of its population. This eruption is estimated to have killed millions of people around the world directly or indirectly. The gas clouds caused crop failures in Europe, drought in India, and Japan's worst food shortage ever.

The Lay of the Land

Iceland measures 39,769 square miles (103,001 square kilometers), which is slightly smaller than the U.S. state of Kentucky. The island is surrounded by the North Atlantic Ocean. Its nearest neighbors are Greenland to the west and Scotland to the east. Iceland is centered over the Mid-Atlantic Ridge, part of the longest mountain range on Earth. Deep beneath the Atlantic Ocean, the ridge is an unpredictable region of shifting land, earthquakes, and volcanic eruptions.

Iceland can be divided into several regions. Cities, towns, and villages dot the coastline. But the center of Iceland is a high desert plateau, where few people live. Even plants have a hard time surviving in the central region. The land that is not lava rock is covered by ice.

The southwest is the most populated region of Iceland. More than 60 percent of all Icelanders live in this area, which includes the capital, Reykjavík, and several suburbs.

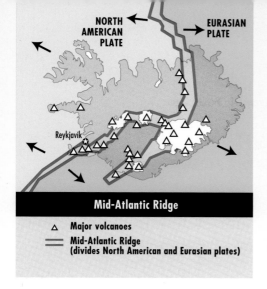

Mid-Atlantic Ridge

△ Major volcanoes
━ Mid-Atlantic Ridge
(divides North American and Eurasian plates)

Cracked Down the Middle

Iceland sits on the Mid-Atlantic Ridge. This is an underwater mountain range where two huge pieces of the earth's outer layer—the North American Plate and the Eurasian Plate—meet. The two plates are slowly moving apart. As they move, Iceland is cracking down the middle. It is separating at a rate of 1 inch (2.5 cm) per year.

Reykjavík means "smoky bay." The name comes from the steam rising from natural hot springs in the area.

Some of Iceland's most rugged land is in the south. This region has several active volcanoes, including Hekla and Katla. Coastal beaches are made of gritty black lava sand and rubble deposited by glaciers.

A string of volcanic islands, called the Vestmannaeyjar, lies just off the southern coast. The islands have steep, sheer cliffs that drop down into the sea.

In 1963, scientists watched the emergence of a new island in the Vestmannaeyjar. Lava poured from a volcanic vent and built the island of Surtsey from the ocean floor up. Today, Surtsey is still in the early stages of acquiring plant and animal life. It is home to sixty types of plants and ten species of nesting birds.

Heimaey is the largest island of the Vestmannaeyjar and the only one on which people live. Helgafell, the volcano that originally formed Heimaey, erupted in 1973. It spewed lava for more than five months. By the time it stopped, one-third of the town on the island was covered by lava.

Iceland's Geographic Features

Area: 39,769 square miles (103,001 sq km)

Largest City: Reykjavík, population 136,354 (2012 est.)

Highest Elevation: Hvannadalshnúkur, 6,952 feet (2,119 m) above sea level

Lowest Elevation: Sea level, along the coast

Longest River: Thjórsá, 143 miles (230 km)

Largest Glacier: Vatnajökull, 3,100 square miles (8,100 sq km), and 3,300 feet (1,000 m) thick

Largest Hot Spring: Deildartunguhver, yields 50 gallons (190 L) of water per second

Most Active Volcano: Grímsvötn

Most Powerful Geyser: Great Geysir, spouts 200 feet (60 m) into the air

Largest Lake: Thingvallavatn, 32 square miles (83 sq km)

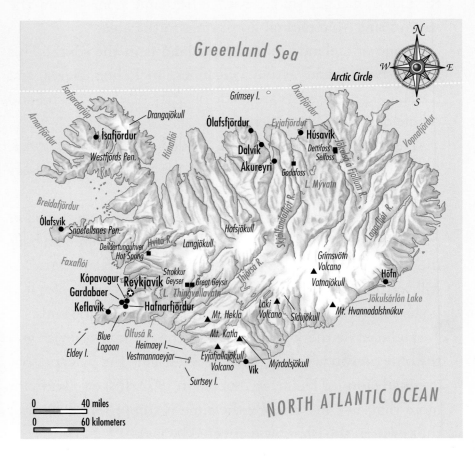

West Iceland has dramatically different scenery from southern Iceland. It is the farming district of Iceland. In this area, the coast rambles around bays and in and out of fjords— long, narrow inlets with steep sides. Visitors can hike up the steep slopes of the Snaefellsnes Peninsula or walk the tan-and-black sand beaches that rim the fjords.

The Westfjords is a rugged peninsula in Iceland's northwest. The region features a jagged coastline with broad beaches, narrow inlets, and rocky cliffs. This is the land closest to Greenland. When thick winter ice covers the North Atlantic, polar bears have been known to walk across from Greenland for a visit to Iceland's northwest villages. Other than Ísafjördur, a town of about 2,600 people, the Westfjords' main inhabitants are millions of seabirds that nest on the sheer cliffs.

After a 1973 volcanic eruption, lava covered much of the town on Heimaey. Only one person was killed in the eruption.

The northern region of Iceland lies just south of the Arctic Circle. The climate is not as bleak as one would imagine. The region boasts relatively mild winters and long, sun-filled summer days. It is warmer and drier in the north of Iceland than in the west and southwest during the summer. The north is the land of glaciers, and many glaciers cap the northern mountains and spread into valleys. Stunning waterfalls, including Dettifoss and Selfoss, are fed by mountain streams and plunge into deep, rocky gorges.

Vatnajökull glacier covers much of the eastern region of Iceland. Small fishing villages are scattered along the coast, but transportation from the villages to other parts of the island can be difficult because the glacier blocks land travel.

Hornstrandir Nature Reserve

Only the most determined trekker ventures into the Hornstrandir Nature Reserve in the Westfjords. The reserve provides no services for visitors—not even a restroom—and visitors must take out every bit of trash they take in. The area was established as a nature reserve in 1975. About 260 types of ground-hugging wildflowers, mosses, and ferns thrive in the reserve. The top predator in the area is the Arctic fox, which preys on the abundant nesting seabirds and field mice. Common birds at the reserve include guillemots, skuas, and razorbills. Trekking tours are done only in the summer, and during this season the sun is up about twenty-two hours a day. This is why one of the treks through Hornstrandir is billed as "eight days and no nights."

Vatnajökull National Park covers all of Vatnajökull glacier and the surrounding area. Iceland's highest peak, Hvannadalshnúkur, is in this park. It reaches 6,952 feet (2,119 meters).

Iceland's mountains are volcanic in origin. Ribbons of hardened lava and deep layers of volcanic ash mark the landscape. Eastern Iceland also features tuyas, steep-sided, flat-topped mountains that form when lava oozes out beneath a thick glacier.

Hikers make their way along the cliffs in the Westfjords to see the nesting birds.

Thundering Falls

Dettifoss, Iceland's largest waterfall, stretches across 330 feet (100 m) in Vatnajökull National Park. At Dettifoss, water from melting glaciers tumbles over a 144-foot (44 m) cliff at a rate of 17,657 cubic feet (500 cubic m) per second. Surrounded by three other waterfalls, the stunningly beautiful Dettifoss is as loud as thunder.

Rivers and Lakes

All of Iceland's rivers are short and cannot be navigated by ship. The longest river is the Thjórsá, which runs 143 miles (230 km) and empties in the south. The Thjórsá begins in the Hofsjökull glacier. The Ölfusá carries the greatest amount of water of any river in Iceland. It supports a large salmon population, and the fishing attracts many tourists.

Thawing glaciers feed the Ölfusá River in southwestern Iceland.

Iceland has sixty-seven lakes and many more smaller ponds. The Icelandic suffix for lake is *vatn*, so Thingvallavatn, the country's largest natural lake, means Thingvalla Lake. The deepest lake, Jökulsárlón, is fed by Vatnajökull glacier. This lake, complete with its own icebergs, has been featured in four movies, including two James Bond films.

Glaciers and Geysers

Water in the form of ice covers part of Iceland. In other areas, scalding water and steam spew up from the ground. Iceland is a land of glaciers and geysers.

Glaciers cover just over 10 percent of Iceland, or about 4,400 square miles (11,400 sq km), but they affect a much larger area than that. Runoff from melting glaciers creates most of Iceland's rivers. The movement of the glaciers plows across the land, carving out lakes and valleys. Glacial water pours into the nation's lakes. On occasion, a glacial flood sweeps across the land, washing away everything in its path.

Below Iceland's surface, water boils and bubbles. There are hundreds of hot springs, many large enough to heat entire

Iceland's Largest Glacier

Vatnajökull glacier covers 8 percent of Iceland and is the largest glacier in Europe by volume. The ice has an average thickness of 1,300 feet (400 m), which is just a bit shorter than the Empire State Building in New York City. Vatnajökull holds nearly twice as much ice as North America's Lake Ontario has water.

Vatnajökull is nearly nine times larger than Iceland's next largest glacier by area, Langjökull. It contains fifteen times the amount of ice as another large glacier, Hofsjökull. Langjökull and Hofsjökull are not small glaciers, but compared to them Vatnajökull is absolutely massive.

cities. Deildartunguhver hot spring produces 50 gallons (190 liters) of nearly boiling water per second. Hot water from Deildartunguhver heats homes in the towns of Akranes, 39 miles (63 km) away, and Borgarnes, 21 miles (34 km) away.

Many hot springs also have geysers, nature's water fountains. The Great Geysir, east of Reykjavík, began spouting in 1294. For centuries, it sent plumes of water 200 feet (60 m) high. Then, in the past hundred years, the Great Geysir became less energetic. It entered a dormant state. Suddenly, in June 2001, the geyser woke up and spit water 130 feet (40 m) into the air. Today the geyser erupts a couple of times daily, but the fountain reaches only about 33 feet (10 m) high.

A slightly more reliable geyser is Strokkur, which spits water 66 feet (20 m) high about every five minutes. The entire area seems to smoke, as vents release steam on a continual basis.

Looking at Iceland's Cities

Reykjavík, the capital of Iceland, is also its largest city, with a population of 136,354. Most of Iceland's other cities are in the Reykjavík area.

The nation's second-largest city, Kópavogur (top left), has a population of 30,779. Located just south of Reykjavík, Kópavogur is a mix of industrial and residential areas. Iceland's tallest building, Smáratorg Tower, is located in the center of the town. Kópavogur has excellent sports facilities, including an open-air heated swimming pool and indoor tennis courts.

Hafnarfjördur (above), which has a population of 26,099, is a suburb of Reykjavík and a busy industrial town. Each May, the town holds the Bright Days Festival, honoring Iceland's sailing history.

Akureyri (bottom left) is home to 17,754 people. Located in northern Iceland, Akureyri is the largest town outside the Reykjavík area. Akureyri is both a fishing town and an education center.

Iceland also has bubbling mudflats, which are as hot as geyser water. Despite signs warning people to keep their hands away from these steaming and bubbling areas, at least half a dozen tourists each year have to be treated for burns from geysers and mudflats.

Thousands of tourists visit Strokkur Geyser every year. Strokkur means "churn" in Icelandic.

Aurora Borealis

One of the most fabulous light shows on earth is free for Icelanders. It is the aurora borealis, or the northern lights. Often during the winter, bands of green, red, and purple lights dance across the night sky. The lights are caused by electrically charged particles from the sun that reach the earth's magnetic field. As the particles travel to the poles, they release energy in the form of light.

Bring a Raincoat

With a name like Iceland, visitors sometimes expect the nation's weather to be freezing at all times. This is not true. The island is warmed by the Gulf Stream, a current of warm water that flows from the Caribbean Sea and the Gulf of Mexico across the Atlantic. Iceland is far greener and warmer than Greenland, its neighbor to the west.

Winters are long, dark, and cold. Snows can fall as early as September in some places and still be melting when the summer sun crosses the sky. However, the coastal waters keep Iceland's most populated areas reasonably warm, considering how far north the country is.

Winter temperatures in Reykjavík rarely drop below 14 degrees Fahrenheit (–10 degrees Celsius). Strong winds whip against Iceland's mountains and rebound with plenty of rain and snow. During the winter, Reykjavík rarely has a month with three completely clear, precipitation-free days. July is even worse. Gales off the North Atlantic blow and bluster, and the locals grit their teeth waiting hopefully for one completely rain-free day.

It rains an average of 148 days a year in Reykjavík. That's almost every other day.

Iceland's highest recorded temperature was 86.9°F (30.5°C) in 1939 on the southeastern coast. The lowest temperature was –36.4°F (–38°C) in 1918 at Grímsstadir in the northeast. Temperature records for Reykjavík include the high temperature of 76.6°F (24.8°C) on August 11, 2004, and the low temperature of –12.1°F (–24.5°C) on January 21, 1918. Midday summer temperatures average 54°F to 59°F (12°C to 15°C).

Precipitation varies greatly from region to region. Reykjavík receives an average of 31.5 inches (80 centimeters) of rain and snow per year. Along the southwest coast and the Vestmannaeyjar, precipitation may be as much as 65 inches (165 cm) for a year. That area experiences fog about seventy days a year. Away from the coast, snow is possible throughout the year.

Summer in Iceland sees many hours of daylight. Winters are equally dark. Grímsey Island is the only portion of Iceland that is actually on the Arctic Circle. There, summer days do not end. For most of Iceland, summer days range from twenty to twenty-two hours long. In the deepest winter, Icelanders enjoy only four hours of daylight.

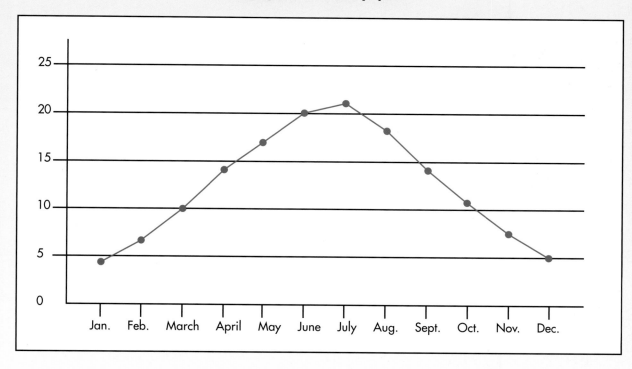

Daylight Hours in Reykjavík

Teeming
with Life

Iceland is home to 60 percent of the world's puffins. Though these orange-beaked, orange-footed birds look a bit like penguins, they are not related to them. Puffins mate for life, but each year, the male and female spend most of their time separately at sea. Every spring, puffin partners return to the same cliffs and build a burrow in the rocks. The female lays one egg, and both the male and female sit on the egg to keep it warm. Once the puffling, the long-awaited chick, is born, the puffin parents take turns fishing and feeding. The puffling has to grow quickly. Come August, it has to fly away.

Some pufflings fly in the wrong direction. In Heimaey in the Vestmannaeyjar, town lights can confuse the young birds. They sometimes crash-land and need a helping hand. Families in Heimaey take to the streets to rescue pufflings. The chicks are collected and placed in warm, padded boxes overnight. The next day, children take the pufflings to the seashore and throw the birds into the air. The pufflings fly away to spend the next eight months at sea.

Opposite: **Puffins are fantastic fishers. They dive to depths of 200 feet (70 m) in search of a meal.**

The End of a Species

Great auks once lived along the coasts of Iceland and North America. Sailors captured them by the thousands, killing them for food and plucking their feathers for pillows. People raided great auk nests for the eggs. By 1800, the last refuge of great auks was Geirfuglasker, a remote island off Iceland. An erupting volcano created a wave of water that covered the island, killing many birds. The remaining great auks fled to Eldey, near the tip of the Reykjanes Peninsula. In 1844, two Icelanders killed the last surviving great auks and smashed their egg. The species became extinct.

A Flurry of Feathers

Puffins are just one of about 80 bird species that nest in Iceland on a regular basis. Another 220 species are summer visitors.

Several members of the auk family, including puffins and guillemots, live in Iceland. These species nest on sheer cliffs, and most lay only one egg per year. Members of the auk family feed on fish and are excellent flyers. The birds all have black backs and wings, and most have white breast feathers.

Other Icelandic birds include fulmars, shearwaters, murres, and petrels, all birds of the open seas. They nest on steep slopes and glide out to sea in search of food. They dive deep into the water to catch fish. Waders and stilts are waterbirds with long legs and sharp, pointed beaks. These birds, like the redshank and the godwit, live along Iceland's beaches. They pluck small creatures from the sand along the water's edge.

Iceland is home to many waterfowl, from stately swans to diving ducks to the red-throated diver. Red-throated divers are only red-throated in the spring, when mating. The rest of the time, they have dull gray-brown feathers. Iceland's only swans are whooper swans. Whoopers breed wherever there are sufficient water plants for nesting material and a pond or lake on which to swim. Iceland's best-known duck is the eider, which is prized for its soft, warm feathers.

Iceland is also home to many songbirds. The most common is the mountain pipit, tiny brown- and gray-feathered birds that live in ground nests and emit single peeps. Pipits eat insects, grasshoppers, crickets, and the larvae of moths and butterflies. Snow buntings are arctic specialists. They are well adapted to the heavy snow and bitter cold.

Fish are the main food of the red-throated diver.

The National Bird

On a sunny summer morning in the arctic region, a mother gyrfalcon swoops down and catches a grouse. This is the first hunt of the day, but one grouse will not be enough to feed her five chicks. She will hunt several times each day for the next few weeks. At eight weeks, the young falcons will be strong enough to leave the nest.

Gyrfalcons nest on cliffs and bluffs along shorelines or by rivers. They are the largest falcons, measuring 20 to 25 inches (51 to 64 cm) long. They feed on ptarmigan, grouse, ground squirrels, and lemmings. Swift flyers, gyrfalcons can snatch prey out of the sky or off the ground.

The gyrfalcon, the largest of all falcons, is Iceland's largest bird of prey and its fiercest hunter. Other birds of prey common to Iceland are small falcons called merlins and two species of owls. Merlins live along the coast in summer and fall. They are swift flyers, gliding along at about 3 feet (1 m) above the ground and startling other birds into taking flight. As the birds flee, the merlins swoop to capture them.

Short-eared owls and snowy owls live in northern Iceland. Short-eared owls are night hunters, feeding on mice, ground squirrels, and rats. Bright white snowy owls must eat eight to ten mice a day to survive. They will eat any animal they can catch. The owls are excellent hunters and help keep down the rodent population.

Not Many Mammals

Before humans settled Iceland, its largest mammal was the Arctic fox. These foxes, which feed on ground birds and rodents, have brown fur in the summer. The fur turns white in the winter, so the foxes blend in with the snow and are protected from other predators.

Marine mammals are common to Iceland's waters. Harbor seals, more common than gray seals, move onto Icelandic beaches to have their pups. They number in the tens of thousands. Minke whales and fin whales frequent Icelandic waters, as do many dolphin species and harbor porpoises. About five thousand orcas live in small groups, called pods, in the waters surrounding Iceland.

Harbor seals sometimes spend days at sea feeding. They return to shore to rest.

One reason so many marine mammals live near Iceland is the abundance of fish in the waters there. Schools of cod, bluefish, whiting, haddock, char, and capelin swim in the waters. Sole, halibut, plaice, and turbot live along the ocean floor.

Growing on the Land

In Iceland, plants hug the ground and have a short life span. They go from seed to flower to seed within two or three months. Most of the nation's five hundred flowering plants came from Europe. Some were brought by humans, while oth-

Wildflowers brighten the landscape on a cloudy day in the Westfjords.

The National Flower

In 2004, a poll of Icelanders determined the country's national flower. The winner was the mountain avens. These delicate flowers bloom on short stems. Each bloom has eight petals, with colors varying from white to cream to yellow in the center.

ers came as seeds carried by the wind, the sea, or birds. Shrubs that produce berries grow well on the soggy land. Crowberries and blueberries are common, as are bog whortleberries.

When humans first arrived in Iceland, much of the coastal land was covered with birch forests. The people cut down the trees for lumber and cleared the stumps to make room for farming. Today, few small groves of birchwood remain. Juniper is the only native cone-bearing tree. Reforestation programs are in place in many parts of Iceland. People are planting hardy pines and hardwoods from other cold regions.

When the spring sun melts the snow, wildflowers begin to bloom. Fields are filled with fluffy, white Arctic cotton grass that turns toward the sun. Harebells create a lush, pale blue carpet on the open land. Brilliant red Iceland poppies line roadsides. In marshy regions, golden marigolds thrive beside water forget-me-nots and purple alpine marsh violets.

Iceland has more than six hundred kinds of moss. Mosses are the first plants that take hold in lava fields. The species called Iceland moss is brown, cushiony, and well suited to growing in harsh environments. Until about a hundred years ago, Iceland moss was commonly used in making bread, soups, and hot cereal.

Delicate, lacy ferns are found among the marshlands and near hot springs. Lady ferns grow beside spiky holly ferns. One of the most unusual fern species is the common moonwort. This tiny fern has cuplike leaves and a thick stem covered with small seedpods.

Mushrooms grow wild in the wetter regions of Iceland. Of the 550 varieties of mushrooms that grow in Iceland, few are poisonous, and none are deadly. Icelanders go mushroom picking on early autumn weekends.

Mushrooms are common in Iceland.

Conservation

Iceland has less pollution than most countries, but it still must deal with conservation issues. The country has very little topsoil, the fertile soil in which crops can grow. Soil erosion poses a major problem. Trees, grasses, and other plants help hold the soil in place. Since settlement, humans have cut down 95 percent of Iceland's trees. Half of all plant matter has been cleared, cut, or destroyed. This leaves the soil with little protection from the wind, rain, and shifting glaciers. Topsoil blows away, is carried by rushing rivers, and is scoured by glaciers. To solve this problem, Icelanders are replanting ground-hugging plants and trees that hold the topsoil in place.

Iceland also needs to protect its fisheries. In the 1980s, Iceland enjoyed record-breaking cod catches. North Atlantic cod stocks were overfished and in danger of disappearing altogether. Iceland's government began setting limits on how many of each kind of fish each fishing boat can catch.

Iceland has set up three national parks: Thingvellir, Snaefellsjökull, and Vatnajökull. Vatnajökull is Europe's largest national park, at 4,633 square miles (12,000 sq km). This park covers 13 percent of Iceland's total area. In addition, Iceland has established eighty nature preserves. Many of the nature preserves protect hot springs, lakes, geysers, waters that support marshes, and a wide range of bird life.

Tourists travel to Vatnajökull National Park to see glaciers, climb mountains, and kayak in lakes.

Past and Present

N O ONE KNOWS EXACTLY WHEN HUMANS FIRST arrived in Europe, Asia, or North America. But this is not the case for Iceland. Its history is fully recorded, from the first sighting of it to the first settlers.

A Greek explorer named Pytheas wrote of a remote island that he called Ultima Thule, Latin for "farthest north," in the fourth century BCE. Pytheas was trying to find out how far north the world stretched. His Ultima Thule was six days' sail north of Great Britain, and a one day sail shy of what Pytheas believed was the "end of the world." Based on his description of the island and its location, historians believe he must have been describing Iceland.

Settlement on the island did not begin until the eighth century CE. The first settlers were Irish monks looking for a place they could pray without interruptions. Iceland had no humans, so it was perfect. Monks were still in Iceland when, in the mid-800s, Norseman Hrafna-Flóki arrived in the area now called the

Opposite: **Ingólfur Arnarson, a Norseman who arrived in Iceland in 874, is called the island's First Settler.**

Early Settlement

— Route of Ingólfur Arnarson, 870–874

Westfjords. His plans to settle in the region were never realized. Winter there was even harsher than in Norway, which led him to call the land Ísland, or Iceland.

Permanent Settlements

True settlement began with Ingólfur Arnarson, whom Icelandic history books call the First Settler. Ingólfur arrived in Iceland in 874 CE from Norway and established a homestead in the southwest, near present-day Reykjavík. After that, Norse settlers began sailing into Iceland's many fjords, bays, and coves. Some historians believe that Norway's poor economy

Finding the Right Spot

When Ingólfur Arnarson, the First Settler, approached Iceland in a Viking ship, he had to decide where to settle. To do this, he heaved the pillars of his high wooden seat overboard. He would settle where the pillars drifted ashore. This spot became Reykjavík.

and shortage of land drove the Norse, who were then called Vikings, to settle Iceland. The Age of Settlement lasted from 874 to 930.

Much of what is known of the early settlement of Iceland comes from *Landnámabók* (*The Book of Settlements*). It describes Iceland's settlement and lists some of its Norse settlers.

In 930, settlement chieftains met at Thingvellir. This is considered the first Althing, or Icelandic parliament. It was the beginning of Iceland's government.

About twenty-five thousand people lived on the island at the time. Large numbers of Icelanders attended the Althing meetings. At these meetings, laws were determined. These

Longhouses

Each Viking community lived basically in one home, called a longhouse. Viking longhouses in Iceland often had stone foundations. The walls and roof were made of blocks of turf—grasses and the soil beneath them held together by roots. A central fireplace heated the house and was used for cooking. A hole in the roof allowed smoke to escape. Most communities also had baths and saunas that were used throughout the year.

Past and Present **45**

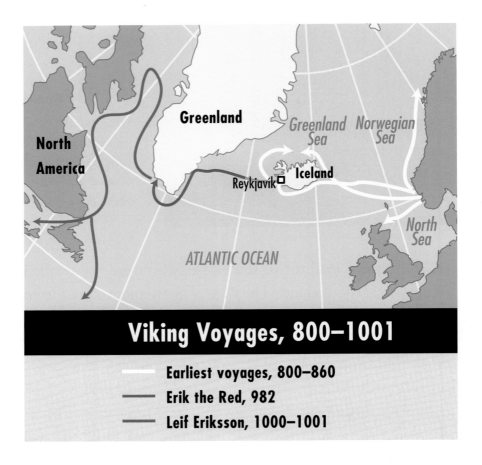

Viking Voyages, 800–1001

— Earliest voyages, 800–860
— Erik the Red, 982
— Leif Eriksson, 1000–1001

laws were memorized and recited by the speaker, the president of the Althing. Four local courts handed down justice, and an appeals court met every year at the Althing. Icelanders dressed elegantly for the meeting, wearing gold jewelry, richly embroidered robes, and decorated helmets. The country's many laws remained unwritten until 1119.

Exploration

One of the great Viking adventure tales is the saga of Erik the Red. Erik went to Iceland with his family because his father was banished from Norway for committing murder. In Iceland, Erik committed murder and was banished from there for three years, so he looked for a new home farther west. Erik founded a colony in a place he called Greenland. He hoped the name would convince others to join him in settling the Greenland colony.

In 1000, Erik's son Leif Eriksson sailed from the Greenland colony. Known as Leif the Lucky, he was the first European known to arrive in North America. Vinland the Good is the name he gave the land, which is in present-day Newfoundland, Canada. Nearly five hundred years later, Christopher Columbus arrived in North America and got the credit for its "discovery."

Erik the Red (right) departed Iceland for Greenland in 982.

Knattleikr

Life in Iceland was harsh and demanding, and Icelanders needed entertainment to keep them happy. During the time of settlement, Icelandic men played a ball game called *knattleikr*. This game may have been an early version of football or rugby. It included wrestling opponents, throwing them to the ground, grabbing the ball, and running with it. The actual rules are unknown, but sagas record that one man threw his opponent down so violently "that he skinned his knees and knuckles, and blood was running from his nose."

Changing Society

Iceland's early settlers believed in Norse gods. But by the late tenth century, King Olaf of Norway wanted them to convert to Christianity. Some people converted, but many still practiced their old religion. At the Althing meeting in 1000, the Althing decided that Iceland would become Christian. People would still be allowed to follow their old religion in private, however.

From 1120 to 1230, Iceland was graced with many brilliant writers and poets. This was a golden age of literature for the

Snorri the Storyteller

Snorri Sturluson (1179-1241) is considered one of the greatest of Iceland's storytellers. Snorri's works are still read today. He wrote the *Snorra-Edda*, which teaches budding poets how to write, and *Heimskringla*, sixteen sagas of Norway's kings.

Snorri was not an easy person to get along with. The king of Norway believed that he was a traitor and ordered him to be killed. Snorri was murdered with an axe on September 22, 1241. Although unpopular in his lifetime, Snorri Sturluson is now admired as one of Iceland's greatest writers.

nation. Poetry flourished. The laws of Iceland were written down for the first time. The nation's greatest heroes became characters in stories that continue to be read today.

Iceland Under Norway

In the 1200s, the king of Norway decided to bring all Viking settlements under his power. Norway took control of Iceland in 1262. Every taxpayer paid an annual fee to the king in the form of wool. The Norse leadership in Iceland was weak, and Iceland fell into a period of violence.

From 1274 to 1276, Norway's King Magnus VI established a new legal system for his entire realm, including Iceland. This legal system was fair and effective, and it stood with few changes until the 1800s. The king was the highest legal authority, and lawbreakers answered to the crown for their crimes.

The biggest problem that faced Icelanders was trade. Icelanders needed to buy most of their goods from other countries. They traded salt fish and wool for metal goods, furniture, finished cloth, spices, and other goods Iceland did not produce itself. But Norway limited Iceland's trading and took part of the profits. Norway's king was supposed to make sure that supply ships arrived regularly in Iceland. All too often, however, the ships never came. Icelanders began trading illegally, mostly with England.

Iceland Under Denmark

In 1397, Norway, Denmark, and Sweden united under one king. This arrangement was called the Kalmar Union. Denmark was the dominant power and took over ruling Iceland. Unlike

Norway, Denmark had no need for Iceland's two main products: wool and fish. The country also had little interest in protecting Iceland, leaving it open to repeated raids by pirates.

Despite having no interest in Icelandic products, in 1602 Denmark established a policy that forbade Iceland from trading with other countries. Iceland's trade remained restricted until 1855.

A small church at Núpsstadur in southern Iceland dates back to the 1600s.

The one major change that Denmark made in Iceland dealt with religion. At the time that Norway brought Christianity to Iceland, all Christians were Catholic. Denmark brought Protestantism to Iceland in the form of the Lutheran religion. Many Icelanders protested against becoming Lutheran. Chief among the objectors were Bishop Jón Arason and his sons. Jón and one hundred men took the town of Saudafell in 1550. A battle followed. The Danish won, and Jón and his sons were beheaded. From that time on, converting Icelanders to Lutheranism went smoothly.

Entering the Nineteenth Century

As the eighteenth century drew to a close, Iceland was struggling. The eruption of Laki in 1783 killed ten thousand Icelanders and more than 50 percent of the farm animals on the island. Another 20 percent of Icelanders died from starvation due to problems that arose from Laki's continued eruption. More than forty years of bad weather, extreme cold, failed fishing missions, floods, earthquakes, disease, and shipwrecks followed. Denmark did not provide enough help, and many Icelanders hoped for independence.

Fishers unload cod in Reykjavík. Fishing has been central to Iceland's economy throughout its history.

It seemed that things could not get worse for Iceland, but they did. As the nineteenth century began, the Danish closed down the Althing, replacing Iceland's government with a Danish governor. Meanwhile, Denmark was engaged in the Napoleonic Wars on the side of France and its leader, Napoléon Bonaparte. The United Kingdom was one of the major forces fighting the French. The British navy soundly defeated the Danish in the Battle of Copenhagen in 1801. Six years later, the British bombed Copenhagen and took away all Danish naval ships and more than ninety merchant ships. This cut Iceland off from its ruling country and the trade it needed in order to live. The people of Iceland struggled to survive.

In 1800, Reykjavík was still a small town. Only about six hundred people lived there.

Toward Independence

In the early nineteenth century, nationalism arose among some people in Iceland. They began to think of themselves as Icelanders first, rather than as subjects of the kingdom of Denmark. Some began urging that the Althing be restored. In 1843, the Althing was reestablished as an advisory body, but it could not make laws.

In 1874, the Althing gained the power to pass laws that dealt with issues inside Iceland. This was the first step to real independence. It took thirty more years for Denmark to release its hold on Iceland's government. In 1901, Denmark's government changed to rule by a parliament, which led the way to Iceland gaining the same rights as Denmark.

Two Danish ships sank and another exploded during the Battle of Copenhagen.

Scholar and Statesman

Jón Sigurdsson (1811–1879) led Iceland's independence movement in the nineteenth century. He spent much of his adult life in Copenhagen, Denmark, where he had attended the University of Copenhagen. Jón knew the Danish king, Christian IX, and spoke with him about restoring the Althing.

When the Althing began again, Jón was chosen as a representative. He promoted agriculture and the use of more advanced fishing techniques. Jón became speaker of the Althing. He returned to Copenhagen and worked to ensure that Iceland would become an independent nation.

In 1904, Iceland began a fourteen-year period of home rule. Change came like an explosion. Telephone service began in 1906. Iceland connected to Europe by telegraph cable. Education became mandatory in all towns and villages. This led to a building boom, as schools sprang up across the country. Fishing vessels, formerly powered by sail, became motorized, making fishing more productive. Labor unions formed, and women got the right to vote in elections. Finally, on December 1, 1918, Iceland gained its independence.

World War II

For the next 22 years, Iceland was free in all matters except foreign relations. In that area, Iceland followed Denmark's lead. In 1940, Germany marched into Denmark. With Germany occupying Denmark, communication between

Denmark and Iceland ended. Within a month, British forces occupied Iceland. In 1941, the defense of Iceland became the responsibility of the United States. The U.S. Army set up a base supported by sixty thousand troops. The United States maintained a military base in Iceland until 2006.

World War II changed Iceland's attitude about its association with Denmark. In 1944, the Althing voted to cut ties with Denmark and become a republic. June 17, 1994 (the anniversary of Jón Sigurdsson's birthday), became Iceland's National Day. Sveinn Björnsson served as Iceland's first president.

Recent Times

Fisheries are an important part of Iceland's economy. With nine out of ten people employed in the fishing industry, Iceland is committed to protecting its ocean waters. In 1975, Iceland

General George C. Marshall (front, center) inspects U.S. troops in Iceland in 1942.

extended its fishery limits to 200 miles (320 km), which led to a dispute with the United Kingdom. The British did not recognize Iceland's right to expand its territorial waters, and British fishers continued to fish in Iceland's waters. The Icelandic Coast Guard cut British fishing nets. Frigates, trawlers, and tugboats rammed each other, and the relationship between the two nations became heated. Tensions in the "Cod War" remained high for seven months before an agreement was reached. In the end, Britain agreed to Iceland's expansion, and Iceland allowed British fishers to temporarily catch fish in Iceland's waters.

An Icelandic gunboat speeds past a British navy boat during the "Cod War" of 1975 to 1976.

In 1980, Vigdís Finnbogadóttir became the first woman elected president of a republic. She was also the first elected female head of state in the world. Vigdís served four terms as president, retiring in 1996.

Financial disaster struck Iceland in 2008. While the rest of the world slipped into a recession, Iceland suffered a near collapse. The government seized partial control of the country's third-largest bank and guaranteed that Icelanders with money in the bank would not lose their savings or investments. Within a few months, the government took complete control of Iceland's top three banks. The government had to borrow $2.1 billion. After that, prices soared and unemployment rose to nearly 10 percent. Facing financial ruin, the government collapsed and elections were held. The new prime minister, Jóhanna Sigurdardóttir, had to deal with Iceland's struggling economy.

To improve the economy, Iceland applied to join the European Union (EU). The EU is an economic and political union with twenty-seven member nations. People who live in the EU can move freely from one nation to another. And most of these nations use the same currency, the euro. Iceland is still waiting to hear if they are going to be accepted. Until then, Icelanders continue to work to make their nation strong again.

Vigdís Finnbogadóttir (left), the world's first female head of state, met with British prime minister Margaret Thatcher (right), the West's first female head of government, in 1982.

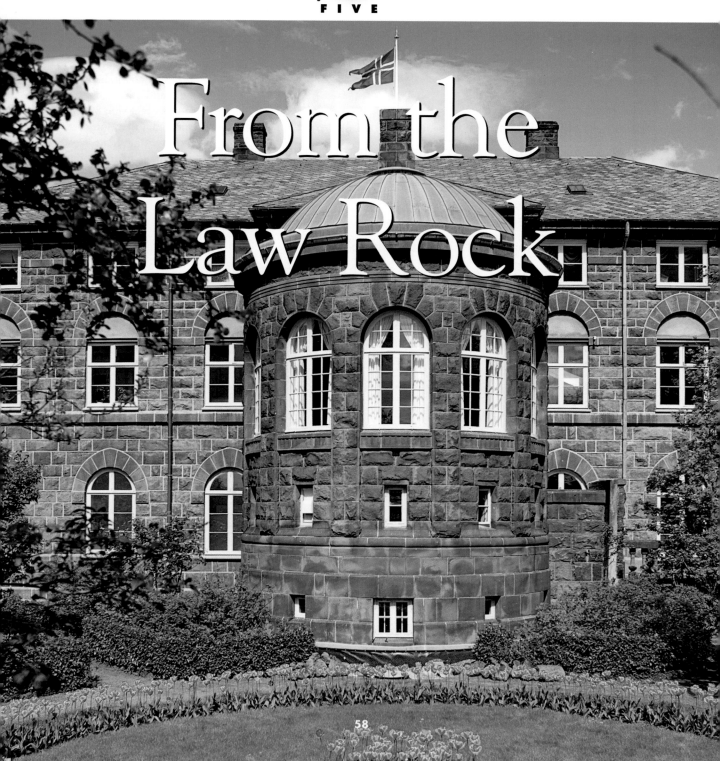

CHAPTER FIVE

From the Law Rock

ICELAND'S FIRST GOVERNMENT BEGAN WITH THE FIRST Althing. That government, called a commonwealth, ran from 930 to 1262 and met at Thingvellir. At the center of the government was the Lögberg, the Law Rock. The speaker of the Althing was chosen by its members and had to know all the laws. Each year, he stood on the Lögberg and recited one-third of the laws of Iceland aloud. After three years, he had recited the entire legal code.

The speaker was not the only one who could speak from the Law Rock. Anyone could stand on the Law Rock and speak to the Althing. Everyone had an equal voice. Today, the speaker of the Althing is still chosen by the members and controls each meeting.

Iceland's Constitution

On June 17, 1944, Iceland became an independent country run under its own constitution. The constitution lists the responsibilities and obligations of the government, as well as the rights and freedoms guaranteed to Icelandic citizens. The

Opposite: **The Althing meets in a nineteenth-century stone building in Reykjavík.**

Icelanders take an active interest in their government. Sometimes this means protesting in front of the parliament building.

people are free to follow their chosen religion. They vote for their leaders and must follow the laws of their land. Citizens have the right to a speedy trial and a jury of their peers. Police cannot search a person's home without a warrant or arrest anyone without just cause.

Like the United States and Canada, Iceland has three branches of government: executive, legislative, and judicial. The executive branch works with the legislative branch to pass and enforce laws. The legislative branch is the Althing, a one-house lawmaking body. The judicial branch reviews laws and hears trials of people accused of breaking laws. Iceland's voters elect all members of their government except Supreme Court judges, who are appointed by the president.

The Executive Branch

The executive branch of Iceland's government includes both a chief of state, called a president, and a leader of the government, called a prime minister.

The president is elected every four years. The president and the legislature have joint responsibility for passing laws. Laws begin as bills in the Althing and are passed on to the president to be signed into law. The president also agrees to treaties with other nations.

The prime minister is the leader of the party that has the most representatives in the Althing. If no party has a clear majority, two or more parties join together to form a government. This is called a coalition. A person may continue to be prime minister as long as his or her political party continues to win the general election, which is held at least every four years. The prime minister's main job is to coordinate efforts of all legislators to set policies on issues affecting the country.

Prime Minister

Jóhanna Sigurdardóttir (1942–) has been prime minister of Iceland since 2009. A former union organizer, Jóhanna entered politics in 1978, when she was elected to the Althing. Her first role as a minister was in the office of social affairs. A member of the Social Democratic Alliance, Jóhanna leads a coalition between the Social Democrats and the Left-Green Movement. In 2012, she was Iceland's longest-serving member of the Althing.

A meeting of the Althing

A cabinet of ministers advises the prime minister on specific policy areas. There are currently nine ministers in Iceland's cabinet. They are in charge of welfare; finance; industry, energy, and tourism; foreign affairs; fisheries and agriculture; education, science, and culture; environment; business; and the interior. The political parties in the coalition select ministers from among their leaders. If there are two parties in a coalition government, the ministers are chosen from both parties.

The Legislative Branch

The Althing is the legislature of Iceland. It has sixty-three members. One of the first jobs that must be handled when the new session of the Althing opens is the election of the speaker. The speaker plans the meetings and oversees the work of the legislature's committees. The speaker arranges for questions to be asked, resolutions and declarations to be made, and reports to be read in

Iceland's National Anthem

"Lofsöngur" ("Song of Praise") is the national anthem of Iceland. Sveinbjörn Sveinbjörnsson composed the music, and Matthías Jochumsson wrote the lyrics. The song was written in 1874 to commemorate the one thousandth anniversary of the beginning of Norse settlement of Iceland. It was adopted as Iceland's official anthem in 1944.

Icelandic lyrics

Ó, gud vors lands! Ó, lands vors gud!
Vér lofum thitt heilaga, heilaga nafn!
Úr sólkerfum himnanna hnýta thér krans
Thínir herskarar, tímanna safn.
Fyrir thér er einn dagur sem thúsund ár
og thúsund ár dagur, ei meir:
eitt eilífdar smáblóm med titrandi tár,
sem tilbidur gud sinn og deyr.
Íslands thúsund ár,
Íslands thúsund ár,
eitt eilífdar smáblóm med titrandi tár,
sem tilbidur gud sinn og deyr.

English translation

Our country's God! Our country's God!
We worship thy name in its wonder sublime.
The suns of the heavens are set in thy crown
By thy legions, the ages of time!
With thee is each day as a thousand years,
Each thousand of years, but a day.
Eternity's flow'r, with its homage of tears,
That reverently passes away.
Iceland's thousand years!
Eternity's flow'r, with its homage of tears,
That reverently passes away.

The design of Iceland's Supreme Court building was determined by a national competition in 1993.

the main chamber. No bill can be voted into law until it is cleared by a committee and read three times in the main chamber.

The Althing meets in the Parliament House. When it first opened in 1881, it housed every part of the government. It also housed the National Library, the Antiquities Collection, and the National Gallery. The Antiquities Collection held the beginnings of what became the National Museum. The University of Iceland began its days with classes on the first floor of the Parliament House. The garden on the parliament grounds was Iceland's first public garden, begun in 1893. Today, members of the Althing have offices in the building so they can quickly go to meetings in the main chamber.

The Judicial Branch

Anyone arrested for a crime in Iceland is entitled to a fair and speedy trial. Trials are public, unless the judge decides to close the court. One reason this might be done is for security.

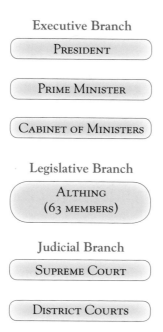

Iceland's Government

Executive Branch

> President

> Prime Minister

> Cabinet of Ministers

Legislative Branch

> Althing
> (63 members)

Judicial Branch

> Supreme Court

> District Courts

The judicial system is made up of district courts and the Supreme Court. There are eight district courts and thirty-eight permanent district court judges.

If a defendant is found guilty in district court, he or she may appeal to the Supreme Court. There are nine justices on the Supreme Court, but they do not all hear every case. Generally, three to five justices are assigned to a specific case. Not every case appealed to the Supreme Court is heard. The case must have some legal reason to be heard in the Supreme Court. Examples of legal reasons are improper defense or failure to follow Iceland's constitution.

A Handshake at Court

Before Iceland's Supreme Court judges begin work each day, they all shake hands. Why? The handshakes are to show that any disagreements or ill feelings from the previous day's work are past, and everyone is facing a new day with a positive attitude.

The Icelandic Flag

Iceland's flag features an off-center cross called a Scandinavian cross. The cross is red with a white outline against a field of blue. Blue represents the sea on which Icelanders have sailed for generations, and white stands for Iceland's many glaciers. The red is both a link to Norway and a reminder that the land was formed from the fires of erupting volcanoes. The flag was adopted in 1915.

Politics in Iceland

Icelanders over age eighteen are allowed to vote, and on average about 85 percent of them vote in every election. Politicians actively compete in elections, and their campaigns are followed closely in newspapers and on radio, television, and the Internet. All major political parties have some representation in local and federal government.

Iceland has five major political parties. The current ruling party is the Social Democratic Alliance, which formed a coalition with the Left-Green Movement. In 2012, these two parties accounted for just over half of the Althing's members. The Social Democratic Alliance favors social equality and a strong, unified Europe. The Left-Green Movement is in favor of protecting the environment and ensuring the rights of women. The other parties in Iceland are the Independence Party, the Progressive Party, and the Movement. The Independents are conservative and do not want to be involved in a united Europe. The Progressives promote the needs of the farming community. The Movement wants to reform the government and its laws.

The Capital City

Reykjavík lies farther north than any other national capital in the world. In 2012, it had a population of 136,354. Including the surrounding suburbs, the Reykjavík area is home to about 198,000 people—60 percent of the national population. Most people in Reykjavík are native Icelanders, but about 6 or 7 percent are immigrants. Polish, Filipino, and Danish people are common among the foreign-born of Reykjavík.

Reykjavík is a lively, modern city and a tourist destination. One of the city's top sites is Hallgrímskirkja, Iceland's largest church (below). This modern Lutheran church was designed to resemble basaltic lava flows. The church also includes a tower from which visitors can see all of Reykjavík. Another popular stop is a historical museum called the Settlement Exhibition, or Landnámssýningin, which features a Viking longhouse that dates back more than a thousand years and other artifacts of the early settlement of Iceland.

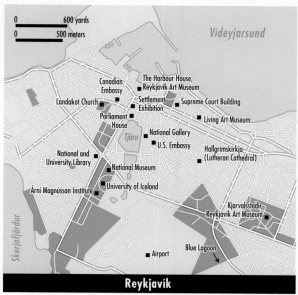

Making Money

IT IS LAMBING SEASON AT THE BRIMNES CATTLE AND sheep farm in northeast Iceland. Arnar and Kjartan, brothers who own the farm, work day and night to ensure the safe birth of the new lambs. Lambs are born in March, when the weather is still brutally cold. The flock consists of three hundred ewes, and many deliver twins.

The newborn lambs and their mothers stay in the barn until the lambs grow and the weather warms up. In the summer, Arnar and Kjartan will drive the sheep into the mountains to feed on natural grasses. When fall comes, all shepherds get together for *réttir*, the sheep roundup. All sheep are herded down from the mountains, identified by owner, and driven home by well-trained sheepdogs.

Opposite: **Icelandic farmers keep about 470,000 sheep.**

Green Living

Iceland may be small, but it leads the world in at least one area: it is rated the cleanest, "greenest" country on Earth. Iceland gets

The Svartsengi power plant uses superheated water from underground to warm the waters in the Blue Lagoon, a popular spa.

most of the energy it uses from geothermal springs, rushing waterfalls, and other renewable resources. The country relies on oil and other polluting fuels only to run cars, trucks, and ships. All other power comes from the forces below Iceland's surface.

Icelanders heat their homes using geothermal energy. In some places, heat from the hot water underground directly heats houses and swimming pools. In other places, the steam from the hot water underground is used to drive electrical generators. Rushing rivers also generate electricity in hydroelectric power plants.

All this "green" energy makes Iceland appealing to companies looking for cheap, abundant power to run their factories. That is why the companies Alcoa and Century Aluminum chose to build major aluminum processing plants in Iceland.

From the Sea

Before refrigeration was common, Iceland's fishing catches were processed into salt fish. Salt preserved the fish so it could

Fish processing is one of the most important industries in Iceland.

be eaten any time of the year, and salt fish was cooked in stews and soups. Today the catch is handled quite differently. Some fish is processed and canned or frozen for sale in supermarkets.

Whaling

During the twentieth century, hunters killed more than two million whales around the world. This left many whale species in danger of being wiped out entirely. The International Whaling Commission banned whaling in 1986. Most countries around the world agreed to the ban, but Iceland did not. Icelanders continued hunting whales. However, under international pressure, Iceland's whaling industry slowed to a halt.

The country has sometimes tried to restart commercial whaling. In 2011, the country allowed whalers to catch 100 minke whales and 154 fin whales. But much of the meat could not be sold. In the past, Iceland sold frozen whale products to Japan. But there is no longer such a large market for whale products there. Whalers in Iceland were left with more than 2,000 tons (1,800 metric tons) of fin whale products in their freezers.

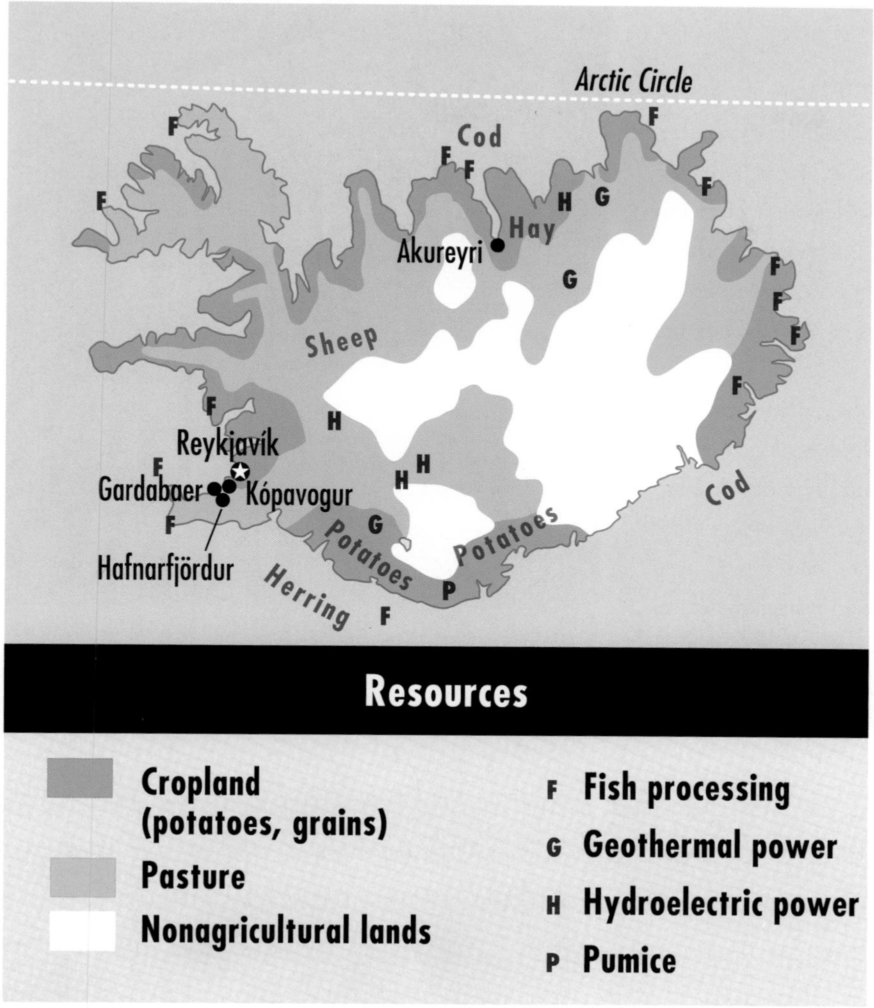
Arctic Circle
Cod
Hay
Akureyri
Sheep
Reykjavík
Gardabaer
Kópavogur
Hafnarfjördur
Herring
Potatoes
Potatoes
Cod
F
G
H
P
Resources
Cropland (potatoes, grains)
Pasture
Nonagricultural lands
F Fish processing
G Geothermal power
H Hydroelectric power
P Pumice

Some fish is packed in ice and shipped, still fresh, to gourmet restaurants. Icelandic cod and haddock are breaded and served as fillets, fish sticks, patties, and fish pies.

Marine resources represent about half of Iceland's economy. The annual catch is about 1 to 2 million tons, and cod is the most heavily fished species. The fishing industry catches about 500,000 tons (450,000 metric tons) of cod, hake, had-

Made in Iceland

There are some products that Iceland is known for, and they just aren't the same in other places. Skyr is a yogurt-like cheese that is a staple of Icelandic diets. It is made and sold in other countries, but people who have eaten the original in Iceland say that other versions just aren't as good. Iceland also claims to have the best hot dogs in the world.

Icelandic wool is heavy, and sweaters made by Icelandic knitters are warm and long lasting. Another typically Icelandic product is an eiderdown comforter, made with the soft, fluffy feathers of the eider duck. Many Icelanders own one, and they last a lifetime. They are extremely soft and incredibly warm. Eiderdown comforters are traditional gifts for children making their confirmation in the Lutheran Church.

Also native to Iceland is scoria. This is a reddish-brown garden gravel that is volcanic in origin.

dock, halibut, sole, redfish, and blue whiting a year. It catches nearly 900,000 tons (800,000 metric tons) of herring and capelin, and 45,000 tons (40,000 metric tons) of shellfish. Iceland also farms salmon, Arctic char, trout, oysters, and mussels.

The fisheries are managed carefully, and each fishing town has specific quotas for fish species. The quotas are set by the Icelandic Ministry of Fisheries, based on stock assessment and scientific advice from the Marine Research Institute.

Manufacturing

Manufacturing in Iceland requires careful planning. Power to run factories is cheap, but Iceland has few resources to use in making products. Natural resources necessary for manufacturing need to be imported. This includes wood, plastic, and metals. Metal processing, particularly of aluminum, is a major industry, but the aluminum must be brought to Iceland from other parts of the world.

Iceland's most valuable manufacturing sector is the production of foods and beverages. This includes everything from making hot dogs (an Icelandic favorite) to canning fish to making soda.

Iceland produces small amounts of computer and electronic equipment, as well as other types of machinery. It also makes clothing and other textiles.

From the Land

Most land in Iceland is not suitable for farming. The growing season is short. Ground crops and grains are the most successful. Hay and other livestock feed are important agricultural products.

Major crops that humans eat include cereal grains such as barley, rye, wheat, and oats. Potatoes, tomatoes, and cucumbers are also grown. Potatoes are a standard field crop, while tomatoes and cucumbers are grown in greenhouses that are heated geothermally.

Farmers in Iceland also raise cattle, sheep, and chickens. There is a small but growing mink industry. Icelandic horses are raised for riding, use on farms, and for sale to other nations. Sweden, Denmark, Norway, and Germany are the main purchasers of Icelandic horses.

Despite the best efforts of Icelandic farmers, Iceland cannot produce enough food for its people. Iceland imports vegetables,

What Iceland Grows, Makes, and Mines

Agriculture (2010)

Hay	2,165,642 cubic meters
Cereal grains (oats, barley, wheat)	13,175 metric tons
Potatoes	12,460 metric tons

Manufacturing (value of goods sold, 2010)

Foods and beverages	US$2,309,310,000
Processed metals	US$1,883,140,000
Chemicals and chemical products	US$100,265,000

Mining (2007)

Pumice	95,000 metric tons

fruit, coffee, and cereals in large quantities. Because the country grows little wheat, it imports cookies, cakes, and other baked goods. There is no source for sugar, so that must be imported either as granulated sugar or in candies and baked goods.

Services

Seventy-three percent of Iceland's people work in services. These include jobs in banking, health care, and education. They may be bank tellers, bus drivers, auto mechanics, nurses, or teachers.

Tourism is a major service industry, accounting for about 5 percent of Iceland's economy. Service workers wait on tables in restaurants and rent hotel rooms to visitors. Most visitors arrive during the summer months and are looking for outdoor adventures. They hike along stunning cliffs, around deafening waterfalls, and through eerie lava fields.

Many people also ride hardy Icelandic horses. These small, muscular horses are very healthy and live a long time. They are the only type of horse in Iceland. Icelanders are not allowed to import any other horse breeds into the country. This helps keep disease from being introduced into the horse population.

Icelandic horses have thick hair that helps keep them warm in the cold weather.

People and Language

B RAGI HAS FINALLY FINISHED HIS SCHOOLING. He graduated from Bifröst University with a degree in business and computer technology. Like many students, he is looking for a job, but he has no intention of returning to Akranes, his childhood home. Bragi is headed to Reykjavík. He is looking forward to the variety of restaurants, nightclubs, and art galleries that only a city can offer.

Opposite: **About 20 percent of Icelanders are under age fifteen.**

Where Icelanders Live

Icelanders are on the move. In the past one hundred years, Iceland has gone from being a mainly rural nation to a mainly urban nation. Just over three hundred thousand people live in Iceland, and more than 90 percent of them live in cities. In fact, most of them live in the same metropolitan area. Reykjavík and the surrounding area are home to nearly two-thirds of all Icelanders. The urban population is increasing at a rate of about 1.5 percent (about 46,000 people) a year.

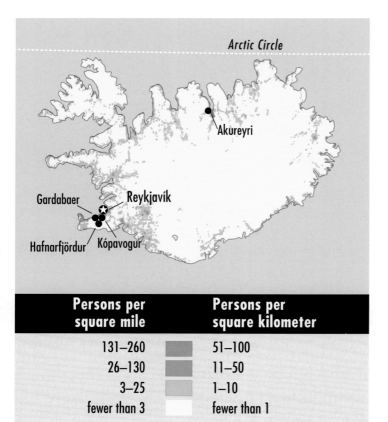

Persons per square mile		Persons per square kilometer
131–260		51–100
26–130		11–50
3–25		1–10
fewer than 3		fewer than 1

Iceland's cities are small in comparison to Reykjavík. Several are suburbs of Reykjavík, including Kópavogur, Hafnarfjördur, Gardabaer, and Mosfellsbaer. Away from the capital, the largest city is Akureyri, with 17,754 people. Cities with populations under 10,000 include Keflavík, Selfoss, and Akranes.

Who Lives in Iceland?

Ninety-four percent of Icelanders trace their heritage back to Norse or Celtic (Scots/Irish) origins. But Iceland's ethnic mix is slowly changing. Six percent of Icelanders come from other ethnic backgrounds. Nearly all foreign-born people or non-Icelanders live in Reykjavík.

Population of Major Cities (2012 est.):

Reykjavík	136,354
Kópavogur	30,779
Hafnarfjördur	26,099
Akureyri	17,754
Gardabaer	10,909

Iceland's Population Shift

Year	Urban Population	Rural Population
1901	23%	77%
1940	67%	33%
1960	82%	18%
1990	91%	9%
2000	92%	8%
2010	93%	7%

The most immigrants by far come from Poland. In 2011, more than nine thousand Poles lived in Iceland. Many of them worked at an aluminum plant in Reydarfjördur, on the eastern coast. The next largest immigrant groups are Lithuanians, Germans, and Danes.

Brightly colored buildings enliven many Icelandic towns.

A Good Life

According to Save the Children Foundation, Iceland is the best place to be a baby and the second best place to be a mother. The advantage is that the government and the population in general support families. Iceland leads all other

Ethnic Iceland

Icelanders	94%
Other Europeans	2%
All Others	4%

On average, women in Iceland have two children.

nations in quality of child nutrition, health facilities for mothers and babies, and social support of mothers.

The birth of a child is a joyous event in Iceland, and family and friends work to help mother and baby. Both fathers and mothers get generous parental leave from their jobs when their babies are born. Universities, churches, and businesses supply on-site child care so that mothers can study or work and also be involved with child rearing.

The Icelandic Language

People who live in Iceland speak at least two languages, Icelandic and English. Many also learn Norwegian, Swedish, Danish, or German. Of all these languages, Icelandic is the least changeable.

Most languages adopt words from other languages. English, for example, relies heavily on Latin and Greek roots, but easily borrows words such as *algebra* (Arabic), *tycoon* (Chinese), and *burger* (German). English has even borrowed an Icelandic word: *geyser*. English also creates new words for new technologies as they develop, such as *astronaut* or *television*.

In the last century, Iceland has had to add many new words to its language. Scholars, language committees, and the general public contribute their ideas about new words. It is a difficult process because Icelanders want to keep their language pure. When Iceland began having telephone service, for example, the language did not have a word for telephone.

Speaking Icelandic

gódan dag	hello or good morning
góda kvöldid	good evening
Hvad heitir thú?	What is your name?
Ég heiti . . .	My name is . . .
Hvad segir thú?	How are you?
já	yes
nei	no
takk	thanks
bless	good-bye
Ég skil thad ekki.	I do not understand.

It was decided to use *sími*, a word that once meant "string" or "thread." Icelanders decided to use the word *thota* for *jet*. It comes from the verb *thjóta*, which means "rush."

During World War II, British and American soldiers in Iceland influenced Icelandic vocabulary. They introduced *jeppi* (Jeep) and *rúta* (bus or route). While Icelanders are happy to borrow words for common speech, they sometimes avoid using them when writing.

Going to School

Iceland is a highly literate country. Ninety-nine percent of the population age fifteen and older can read and write. This level of literacy comes from the emphasis Icelanders put on education. Iceland provides four levels of public schooling: pre-primary; compulsory; upper secondary; and university and college.

Pre-primary school covers children from ages one to six. More than nineteen thousand students attend public pre-

Rock, River, Glacier

Compound words are common in the Icelandic language, particularly when describing place names. The great majority of Icelandic towns, regions, and geological features are compounds of adjectives and nouns used to form a name. Here are some examples:

Term	Meaning	Place Names
Foss	Waterfall	Gulfoss, Dettifoss, Selfoss
Fjördur	Fjord or valley	Ísafjördur, Hvammsfjördur, Vopnafjördur
Jökull	Glacier	Vatnajökull, Hofsjökull, Langjökull
Vatn	Lake	Mývatn, Thingvallavatn
Vík	Bay	Reykjavík, Keflavík, Dalvík

Sjóðandi vatn
boiling water

primary classes. In pre-primary school, children learn how to play with others and follow directions. They also gain basic education skills. Pre-primary school lays the foundation for children to become independent and active members of the community. Teachers encourage creativity and boost self-confidence, as well as work with children to speak clearly.

Compulsory schools are for children from ages six to sixteen. Compulsory schools teach children the typical school subjects including math, language arts, science, history, and foreign languages such as English or German. Students also

Popular tourist sites often have signs in both Icelandic and English.

Pre-primary school is not required in Iceland, but about 97 percent of children attend.

learn about society, living conditions, and environmental issues. Students develop a well-rounded approach to learning, balancing physical wellness with studying arts, sciences, and history. Physically challenged students attend the regular compulsory school, and special accommodations are made to help these students succeed. Students attend classes 180 days a year, with time off for winter and spring holidays and long vacations during July and August.

Any student who has completed compulsory education has the right to enter an upper secondary school. Students at these schools are sixteen to twenty years old. They study academic subjects to prepare them for going on to university. They may also attend a vocational school and learn a trade.

The current university system began in 1911 with the founding of the University of Iceland. There are currently seven higher education institutes. These are open to students who have graduated from the upper secondary school.

Exercise is an important part of the school day in Iceland.

Different higher education schools offer different courses of study. Several schools offer courses in agriculture, for example, but only the University of Iceland offers degrees in language arts. Popular study programs include teacher training, law, economics and business, and agriculture.

Iceland also has an active lifelong learner program. The government offers courses for adults to build computer skills,

Fourteen thousand students attend the University of Iceland, the largest university in the country.

About 62 percent of college students in Iceland are women.

learn new trades, and support current careers. Some of the classes offered are purely for enrichment. They include learning a new language, cooking foreign dishes, and music or art appreciation. Other classes specifically help people advance in their chosen careers. They might include using spreadsheets on a computer or learning advanced agricultural techniques. Regardless of the subject matter, the Icelandic Ministry of Education is determined to provide engaging courses for all students. Age doesn't matter—education does.

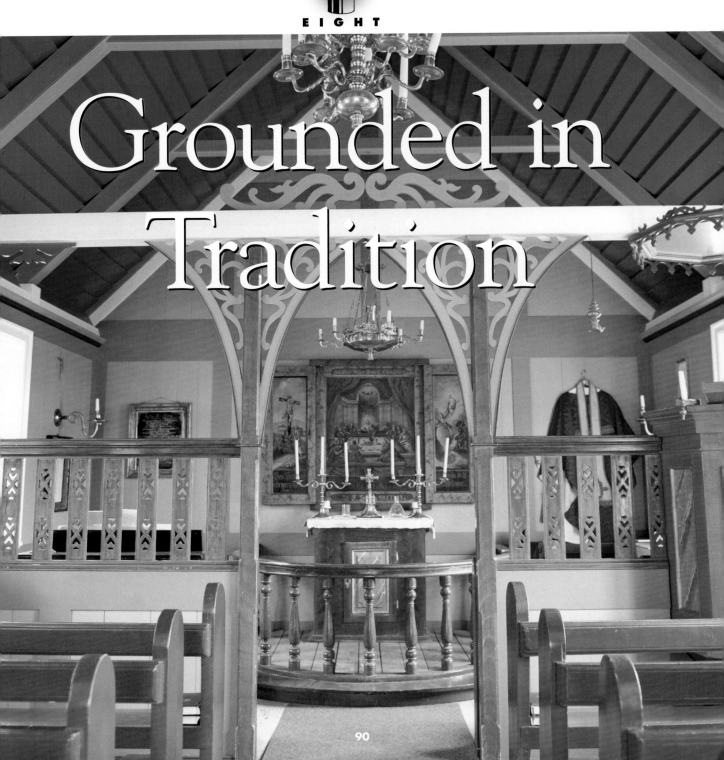

Grounded in Tradition

LÁRA IS APPROACHING HER FOURTEENTH BIRTHDAY. Fourteen is a big year for Icelandic teens. It is the year of their confirmation ceremony in the Church of Iceland. This coming-of-age ceremony is held between Easter and Whitsunday, which is seven weeks after Easter. At the church, Lára will confirm her faith in God. She attends weekly classes to prepare for the service. In addition, Lára's family and friends will gather for a big party.

For the party, Lára will learn how to bake a *kransakaka*, a traditional cake. There will also be a cream-filled sponge cake on which Lára's name and confirmation date are written in chocolate. Lára will also help cook other dishes the guests will eat.

Today many girls being confirmed allow their hair to grow long. They spend the day before confirmation with a stylist, who turns their long hair into waves and braids, decorated with pearls or flowers. During the service, Lára wears a white dress. Along with several other teens, Lára confirms her beliefs and is accepted as an adult member of the church.

Opposite: **Lutherans make up a higher percentage of people in Iceland than in any other country in the world.**

Religion in Iceland (2012)

Church of Iceland (Lutheran)	76.8%
Other Lutheran	5.7%
Roman Catholic	3.3%
Other Christian	2.3%
Paganism	0.6%
Buddhism	0.3%
Other or not specified	6.1%
No religion	4.9%

The Landakot Church in Reykjavík is the largest Catholic church in Iceland.

When the service ends, it is time for the party. Guests give both traditional and nontraditional gifts. Lára's parents give her an MP3 player, and her grandparents give her an eiderdown comforter. The comforter represents Lára's entrance into adulthood.

The Church of Iceland

Icelanders are free to follow the religion of their choice. More than three-quarters of Icelanders belong to the state church, the Evangelical Lutheran Church of Iceland. The head of the church is the bishop, and the current bishop is the Right Reverend Agnes M. Sigurdardóttir. The main church is Hallgrímskirkja in Reykjavík.

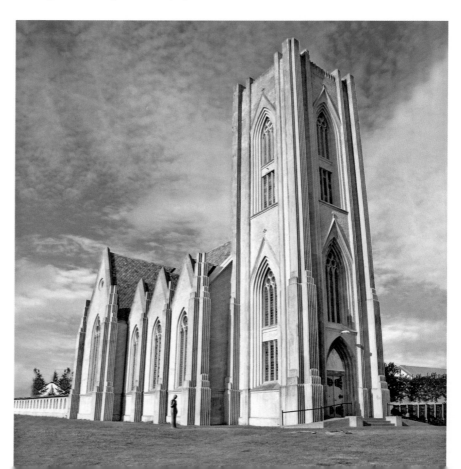

Lutheran priests leaving a church after a service

Lutheran beliefs are founded on the Bible and the teachings of Martin Luther, a sixteenth-century German monk who objected to some Catholic practices. Lutherans participate in a variety of sacraments, or holy rites. The first is baptism, which is blessing a baby in the church. Parents take their child to church, where baptism is a public event. The minister sprinkles water on the baby's forehead and names the child as a child of God. Two close relatives or friends are chosen to be godparents. They commit themselves to helping raise the child as a member of the church.

A second Lutheran rite is penance, the act of being sorry or making up for one's sins. Lutherans confess their sins and ask for forgiveness for wrongs they have committed. Confession may be a silent admission of sin during a church service or a private visit with a minister. In a third rite, Lutherans take part in communion, a ritual symbolic of the breaking of bread at the Last Supper by Jesus Christ and his followers before Jesus's death.

Religious Holidays

The two biggest religious events of the year are Easter and Christmas. Easter season begins with Explosion Day, the day before Lent, which covers the forty days before Easter. It is a time of fasting and prayer. On Explosion Day, Icelanders eat buns stuffed with cream filling. In the afternoon, the family eats salted lamb and split pea soup. The idea is for everyone to eat until they explode because the next forty days will be a time of sacrifice.

Holy Week, the days right before Easter, is important to Icelanders. Easter is a family event. Businesses and schools close for Holy Thursday. On Easter Sunday, children get chocolate eggs from parents and grandparents. Sunday morning the family goes to church together. Relatives get together for lunch or dinner. This is also a fun weekend, and many families go on short trips or go see a movie.

It is traditional for families to decorate the graves of relatives at Christmastime.

During the Christmas season, many Icelanders take part in a walk for peace through Reykjavík.

The Christmas season is called Advent, and begins four Sundays before Christmas. Families take trips to the city and start their Christmas shopping. Christmas lights brighten up the long, dark winter nights. Fun begins December 12 with the arrival of the Yuletide Lads. In old folktales, the Yuletide Lads played tricks and were portrayed scarily. Now, they are depicted more like Christmas elves, and they are said to leave presents in children's shoes.

December 23 is St. Thorlákur's Day. This day honors an Icelandic monk and bishop who lived during the twelfth century. Icelanders decorate their Christmas trees on St. Thorlákur's Day. They also eat a simple dinner such as skate hash, which is a mix of skate (a type of fish), potatoes, and onions.

Religious Holidays

Epiphany	January 6
Explosion Day (Shrove Tuesday)	Day before Lent starts
Ash Wednesday	Start of Lenten season
Holy Thursday	March or April
Good Friday	March or April
Easter Sunday	March or April
Easter Monday	March or April
Ascension Day	May or June
Whitsunday, Whitmonday	May or June
St. Thorlákur's Day	December 23
Christmas Day	December 25

Like Easter, Christmas is a time for family. Parents and children spend Christmas Eve together, eating dinner and opening presents. Christmas Day is the time for grandparents, aunts and uncles, and cousins to get together. The traditional Christmas dinner is eaten at 6:00 p.m. on Christmas Eve. It includes roast game, such as reindeer or ptarmigan, or smoked

The Yuletide Lads

According to Icelandic folklore, the Yuletide Lads are thirteen sons of Grýla the ogre. In these stories, each lad had a particular trick he would play, from slamming doors to stealing sausages to stealing milk from the cows in the shed. Parents sometimes told tales of the lads to scare children into proper behavior. Today, in Christmas season performances and the stories parents tell, the lads are depicted more like Santa Claus. For the thirteen nights before Christmas, the Yuletide Lads are said to leave small presents in shoes that children have left by the window.

Children dressed as elves join a Christmas parade in the Vestmannaeyjar.

lamb. There may also be duck or turkey. Dessert is typically Christmas cake or mince pie. Icelandic Christmas cakes are lemon pound cake with raisins or *vínarterta*, six thin layers of rich almond cake separated by prune filling.

Norse Beliefs

Although few Icelanders still believe in the Norse gods, the Viking tradition is ever present. The connection to Norway and Viking religion is seen daily in the names people choose for their children. For boys, Thor is common, as are Odin, Baldur, and Bragi. Girls' names include Frigg, Eir, Freyja, Nanna, and Sif.

In Norse mythology, the Norse gods were ruled by Odin, the all-father and most powerful of gods. His wife was Frigg, the mother goddess. Each god had a responsibility, gift, or power over humans. Thor was the god of thunder, a powerful warrior, and a child of the all-father. Bragi was the god of poetry, while Freyja was the goddess of love. Just as there were gods of life, there were also gods of death, including Hel (goddess of the underworld), Rán (goddess of the drowned), and Baldur (the dying god).

Odin and his wife, Frigg, were major gods in Norse mythology. Their names remain popular in Iceland today.

The Guardian Spirits

According to an ancient legend, King Harald of Denmark sent a magician to explore Iceland. The magician arrived in Icelandic waters in the form of a whale. He saw that spirits with many powers overwhelmed the land. He went to Vopnafjördur in the east, where he met a huge dragon. To the north, in Eyjafjördur, he came upon a bird so large that its wings spread from one mountain peak to another. In the south, at Breidafjördur, a huge bull waded into the sea to stop the magician's approach. In the region of Reykjanes he came up against a rock giant. These spirits protected Iceland from King Harald, and each is depicted on Iceland's national coat of arms.

Elves, Trolls, and Ghosts

Iceland also has a strong tradition of folk beliefs. These include stories of elves, trolls, and ghosts. Elves are depicted with handsome, humanlike features. Legends claim that elves were the children of Eve, the first woman on Earth. Eve hid the elves from God, but when God found out about them, he declared that elves would remain hidden people forever. Supposedly elves live in hills and cliffs and dress like humans. In surveys, about 5 percent of Icelanders state that they have seen elves, and more than 55 percent of Icelanders believe they exist.

Trolls are giants. They are depicted as strong, ugly, and violent creatures. Trolls are always committed to revenge, and will pay back anyone who does them ill. But they are also generous to those who do them favors. In the past, Icelanders believed that trolls lived on the bird cliffs. It is said that night trolls must return to their cave homes before daylight or they will turn to stone.

According to ancient Norse beliefs, ghosts were spirits of the dead who had gone on to the afterlife but still had a presence on Earth. It was believed that powerful magicians could call ghosts back to life. Today, 41 percent of Icelanders claim to have had contact with the dead. Eighty-eight percent of Icelanders believe it is possible to see people who have died. Traditionally, Icelanders named their children after dead relatives. This kept both the name and the spirit of the dead person alive, and was believed to keep ghosts from haunting the family.

Children play in the cauldron of a troll statue. Troll statues are common throughout Iceland, and troll characters loom large in Norse folklore.

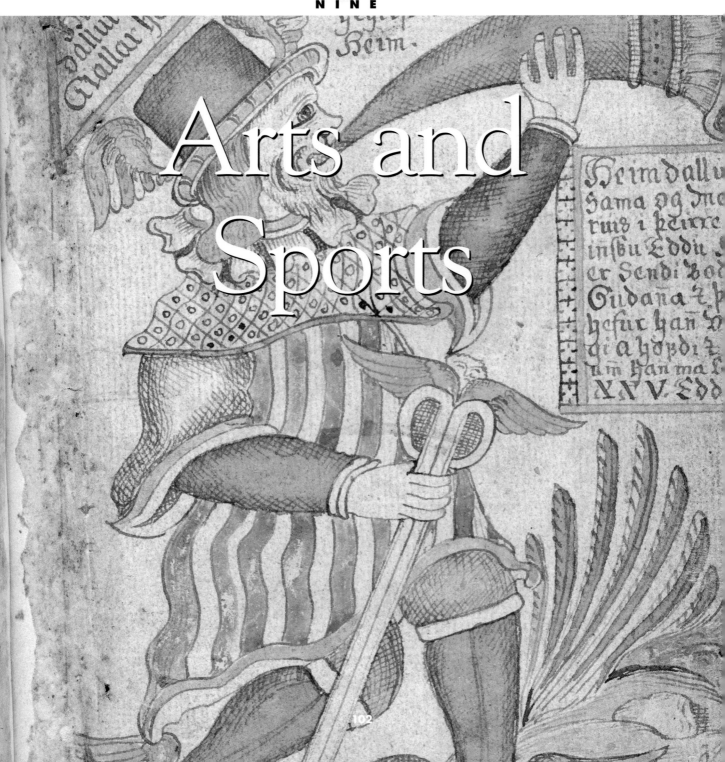

Arts and Sports

AT A TIME WHEN MOST PEOPLE COULD NEITHER read nor write, Icelanders wrote down the tales of their legendary heroes. These tales were both in prose (sagas) and in poetry (Eddic and skaldic), and were composed in Icelandic. The use of Icelandic was unusual, because most people who could read and write were Catholic priests and monks, and they wrote in Latin.

Opposite: **A page from** ***Melsted's Edda*** **shows Heimdall, the watchman of the gods, blowing his horn.**

Sagas

Sagas are heroic, romantic, or historic stories. One of the earliest sagas of Icelanders is *Egil's Saga* about the Viking poet Egill Skallagrímsson. Other sagas of Icelanders are *Gísli Súrsson's Saga* and *Grettis Saga* about the outlaws Gísli and Grettir. *Njal's Saga* is the longest and most famous saga.

All sagas have certain characteristics that tie them into a specifically Icelandic genre. The main characters are very human in their attitudes toward life. Saga characters are basically good people with a few obvious flaws. They get involved in fights, feuds, murders, and mayhem on a regular basis. There is an all-important code of honor, and courage is admired above cunning. There are few perfect heroes, just as there are few absolute villains. The characters stick to the belief that it is better to die well than to live with dishonor.

Some saga manuscripts include ornate decoration.

The Árni Magnússon Institute for Icelandic Studies preserves many important manuscripts.

In the 1700s, a scholar named Árni Magnússon began collecting saga manuscripts. Over the course of many years, he brought cases filled with manuscripts back to Copenhagen, Denmark. They are now housed in the Arnamagnaean Institute at the University of Copenhagen.

Since independence in 1944, the Icelandic government has often talked with Denmark about returning manuscripts. More than 1,800 documents have been given back to Iceland. They are now stored in Reykjavík, at the Árni Magnússon Institute for Icelandic Studies, which was named in honor of the man who originally preserved this valuable link to Iceland's heritage.

Many Icelanders write to pass the long winter nights. Poetry writing is popular and something of an Icelandic tradition. Politicians, teachers, fishers—any Icelander might create a bit of poetry.

Most Icelanders make time for reading in their daily routines. People read everything from ancient sagas to books that have just been written. Among the nation's best sellers are mysteries by Arnaldur Indrídason and modern novels by Halldór Laxness and Einar Már Gudmundsson. Einar's novel *Englar alheimsins* (*Angels of the Universe*) won the Nordic Council Literature Prize in 1995.

Kristín Marja Baldursdóttir's first novel *Mávahlátur* (*The Seagull's Laughter*) was made into a play and film dealing with the reality of women's dreams and longings. In 1996, Steinunn Sigurdardóttir, another popular novelist, won the Icelandic Literary Prize for her novel *Hjartastadur* (*Heart's Place*). The book deals with the difficulties between a single mother and her teenage daughter. Vigdís Grímsdóttir, a poet and writer, enjoys popularity both in Iceland and throughout Europe.

Mysterious Iceland

Arnaldur Indrídason is a journalist and novelist based in Reykjavík. One of Iceland's most popular novelists, Arnaldur is known for his mystery series featuring Detective Erlendur. One of these books, *Mýrin*, was produced as a film under the title *Jar City*. Arnaldur's work has been translated into twenty languages and sells widely throughout Europe.

The works of Steinunn Sigurdardóttir focus on the relationships between people but also include expressive descriptions of Iceland's landscape.

Popular Poetry

In early Iceland, some poems were used to tell a story, honor a hero, or express one's feelings. These are called Skaldic poems. Other poems, called Eddic poems, tell about the Norse gods or heroes from the age of migration. Most Eddic poetry is collected in a manuscript called the Codex Regius. One of the greatest is a poem entitled *Hávamál*, an epic work that supposedly represents the words of Odin, the all-father. Here is a stanza from *Hávamál*:

> *A wise counselled man will be mild in bearing*
> *and use his might in measure,*
> *lest when he come his fierce foes among*
> *he find others fiercer than he.*

Icelanders read more books per person than people in any other country in the world.

The names of several early Icelandic poets are known. Between the 800s and the 1200s, Iceland had about one hundred *skalds*, poets who wrote for Icelandic chieftains and European nobles. In Denmark, Norway, and Sweden, some of these men served as court poets to Scandinavian kings. Many poems from this early era survive. Notable skalds included Bragi Boddason and Egill Skallagrímsson.

In the 1800s, many poets chose to write about independence and freedom. The poet Jónas Hallgrímsson took a

Sjón has written more than twenty books, including novels, poetry collections, and children's books. His work has been translated into twenty-three languages.

radical approach to poetry. He wrote in common language and chose common themes. Jónas's best-known work is *Ísland* (*Iceland*), which honors his homeland and looks forward to an independent future.

Graphic Novels

Many teenagers in Iceland love graphic novels. The nation's largest publisher, Edda-Midlun, publishes at least one graphic novel each season. Many of the most popular graphic novels are illustrated retellings of classic Icelandic sagas. Another popular book is Nanna Árnadóttir's *Zombie Iceland*. This is a somewhat unusual travel guide to Iceland in that it is a tale about zombies that includes footnotes about the history, culture, and food of Iceland, among other interesting information about the country.

Poetry continues to be a popular form of literature among Icelanders. Writing poetry or song lyrics is a pastime for young and old alike. Sigurjón Birgir Sigurdsson, better known as Sjón, is a popular Icelandic poet. He has also written lyrics to songs performed by the Icelandic singer Björk and won the Nordic Council's Literature Prize for his novel *Skugga-Baldur* (*The Blue Fox*).

Some of the paintings of Jóhannes Kjarval depict mythical creatures, while others show nature. This one is called *Lava at Bessastadir*.

Icelandic Art

Danish-trained artist Thórarinn Thorláksson became the first Icelander to exhibit his paintings in Iceland, in the early 1900s. People were so interested in Thórarinn's art that he received a public grant to continue painting. His most famous works were landscapes of Thingvellir. Thórarinn was also highly political, favoring independence for Iceland.

A number of artists followed Thórarinn's lead in being both political and artistic. Among them were Jóhannes Kjarval and Júlíana Sveinsdóttir. Jóhannes, one of Iceland's most famous artists, focused on painting mythical figures, such as elves and trolls. Part of the Reykjavík Art Museum—the Kjarvalsstadir—is named for him. Júlíana was one of Iceland's first well-known female painters. She also designed abstract rugs, for which she won international awards.

Today, Iceland's artists display their work in exhibitions in the National Gallery. Every year, a new group of budding artists show their paintings, textile art, or glass art.

Music

Since Viking times, Icelanders have played instruments and sung music. Singing and dancing are part of most festivals. The musical group Voces Thules specializes in singing Icelandic medieval music.

The Violin Maker

Hans Jóhannsson has a most unusual career. He makes stringed instruments: violins, cellos, violas, and bass viols. Hans learned his craft from his grandfather, and each instrument he makes is unique. He designs each instrument himself. For people interested in purchasing an instrument, there's a two-year wait.

Björk sings in a wide range of styles. She is known for her highly expressive, improvisational singing.

Traditional Icelandic folk dances, such as the *vikivaki*, tell a story. They include arm motions and patterns of steps much like square dancing.

Modern music also thrives in Iceland. Reykjavík has a symphonic hall and orchestra. There are also many popular folk groups, rock bands, and jazz groups.

For a nation with such a small population, Iceland has produced an unusual number of world-class rock musicians. Iceland's best-known musician, Björk Gudmundsdóttir, is a huge international star. Born in Reykjavík in 1965, Björk released her first album at eleven years old. She toured with the Sugarcubes for several years, before going solo in 1992. Like Björk, Páll Óskar Hjálmtýsson—known as Paul Oscar—has a worldwide reputation as a singer and songwriter. Another popular Icelandic band is Sigur Rós. Founded in 1994, Sigur Rós creates eerie music that falls somewhere between rock and new age sound.

The music of Sigur Rós is airy and mysterious.

Icelanders often have fun in the snow.

Sports

Icelanders as a whole are active, busy, and athletic. Many go hiking or biking when they have time off from school or work. In warmer weather, children play soccer or ride horses. In winter, they take part in hockey, figure skating, cross-country skiing, and swimming! Yes, Icelanders swim all year in public pools heated by geothermal energy.

Team sports keep Icelanders of all ages physically fit. Both men and women play soccer, basketball, volleyball, and hand-ball. Many people play golf and tennis.

The oldest organized sporting association in Iceland is the Reykjavík Shooting Association, founded in 1867. The sport involves people shooting rifles and pistols at targets.

Iceland also has professional athletes, although most of them play for soccer teams in Europe. The most famous Icelandic athlete is Eidur Gudjohnsen, a soccer player for AEK Athens football club in Greece. Eidur has also played for Chelsea in England and FC Barcelona in Spain. He has played for Iceland's national team since 1996.

Another sport that draws major fan interest is the World's Strongest Man competition. Two Icelanders, Magnús ver Magnússon and Jón Páll Sigmarsson, have won four times each. The competition requires lifting weights, pulling weighted sleds, playing tug-of-war, and such events as the unusually named Hercules hold, farmer's walk, and duck walk. These might sound simple or easy, but the duck walk requires carrying a 400-pound (181 kilogram) pot, suspended between the legs, over a marked course.

Icelandic Wrestling

There are few sports quite like *glíma*, Icelandic wrestling. Athletes who participate in glíma are carrying on a sporting tradition that stretches back to Viking times. The word *glíma* means "game of joy," and has been practiced for centuries. Wrestlers wear thick belts around their waists and a belt on each thigh. The belts give opponents a place to grip. Both wrestlers begin in an upright position. They move in a circle. One wrestler throws the other to the mat, trying to make the opponent touch hips, chest, or upper legs against the mat. The wrestler who forces the other onto the mat two times is declared the winner.

Family Ties

SIGGA AND HJALTI ARE BUSY HELPING THEIR MOTHER, Margrét, in the kitchen. This weekend is Thorrablót, a mid-winter festival. On the first Friday after January 19, friends and family gather in Margrét's farmhouse for food, drink, stories, and games. Margrét and her children make sure there will be plenty of food to go around.

The traditional dishes served are not for squeamish eaters, but they are foods Icelanders ate centuries ago. On the table will be rotten shark's meat (*hákarl*), dried cod, boiled sheep's head (*svid*), and clotted sheep's blood served in a ram's stomach. There will also be potato salad, mashed rutabagas, and a variety of breads.

The night will be spent telling stories, singing, dancing, and playing games. Thorrablót lasts for hours, with guests making several trips to the food table. The guests leave sometime around 3:00 a.m., and the hosts sink into bed for well-deserved sleep.

Opposite: **A mother and her children enjoy a trip to a geothermal spa.**

Hákarl

During the early settlement of Iceland, food was often scarce. People could not afford to let anything go to waste. Greenland sharks are poisonous when they are first killed. But as the meat ages, it becomes safe to eat. This dish of rotten shark's meat is called *hákarl*.

This is how hákarl is made. A shallow hole is dug in gravelly sand and a piece of Greenland shark is placed in the hole. Then the shark meat is covered with sand and gravel and left to rot for about six to twelve weeks. This is called fermenting, the same process used to make beer and wine. Next, the meat is dug up, cut into thin strips, and hung to dry like jerky. It is ready to be served after the brown crust is scraped off and the meat is cut into small bites. Hákarl has a strong ammonia-like smell and a very fishy taste. It is a traditional Icelandic food to serve at a winter feast.

Holidays

Iceland has a number of public holidays. Labor Day and réttir celebrate Iceland's great tradition of hard work. On Labor Day, May 1, city dwellers flee to the country for a long weekend. The day honors workers, but it is also May Day, a holiday that stretches back to Viking days. The weather is usually good, and people celebrate this day as the end of winter.

Réttir is the annual sheep roundup. In the summer, farmers release their sheep to graze in the mountains. In September, it is time to bring them home again. Sheep have ear tags identifying which animal belongs to which farmer. The sheep are driven down from the hills into a main enclosure. They are identified and collected by their owners, who herd them back to their farms for the winter.

During réttir, farmers collect their sheep from large corrals. It is a festive time.

An interesting "unofficial" holiday is *sólarkaffi*, or sun coffee. This is celebrated in northern Iceland on the first day that the sun returns after sunless winter days. The day changes from community to community, but it is traditional to have friends in for coffee and cake.

National Holidays

New Year's Day	January 1
Holy Thursday	March or April
Good Friday	March or April
Easter Sunday	March or April
Easter Monday	March or April
First Day of Summer	First Thursday after April 18
Labor Day	May 1
Whitsunday and Whitmonday	May or June
National Day	June 17
Commerce Day	First weekend in August
Réttir	September
Christmas	December 25
Boxing Day	December 26

From Birth to Death

Family ties in Iceland are strong, and a family's history is important. It is common to ask, "Who are your people?" when meeting an Icelander for the first time. Genealogy, the study of a family's roots, has become a common hobby among Icelanders.

One of the greatest joys in any family is the birth of a child. Traditionally, it was bad luck to tell a child's name before the baptism, when the child is christened. This was because so many

An Icelandic girl harvests hay. Children who live on farms often help with the work.

infants died soon after they were born. Today Iceland has one of the world's lowest infant mortality rates. Just three out of every one thousand infants die. By the time they are about two or three months old, many babies are christened in the church. The family receives gifts and holds a party to celebrate the child's christening day.

Children are expected to succeed in their main job: being children. Parents expect them to do well in school. Parents and grandparents play active roles in raising the children. They arrange for children to take part in hobbies and sports, and to play musical instruments. Most children read every day, and families plan regular visits to libraries or bookstores to keep a stock of reading materials on hand. Parents teach their children how to play chess, bridge, and other games. During the summer, children eight years of age and older may spend vacation time with relatives who live on farms. There, they get plenty of fresh air and exercise, and they assist their relatives at a time when help in running a farm is needed most.

A boy plays with his grandfather. On average, Icelanders live to age eighty-one.

By the time they are teenagers, children are fairly independent. Teens who live in Reykjavík go out together on Friday nights and stay out late. Teens are expected to hold jobs once they are fourteen years old. They earn their own spending money, do their own laundry, and can cook for themselves.

Young adults are not encouraged to marry early. Many couples date for several years, and engagements tend to be lengthy. Wedding ceremonies are similar to American wedding customs. The bride and groom have attendants, ring bearers, flower girls, and a reception afterward. The bride and groom must be at least eighteen years old. The guests give the newly married couple presents at the reception. Books and artwork are popular gifts.

Some young couples live with their parents, even after they have children. It is a wise move in an effort to save money toward buying a home. Grandparents can provide child care while both young parents are at work.

After a person dies, friends visit the deceased person's family either at home or at a funeral chapel. On the day of the funeral, newspapers print letters and stories written about the deceased person by his or her friends. The actual funeral is held in a church, and family, friends, and co-workers fill the church pews. A minister speaks at the funeral, often telling personal stories about the deceased. Afterward, only the immediate family goes to the cemetery. Family will return to the gravesite on the deceased's birthday and at Christmas to place flowers, candles, or pine branches on the grave.

Icelandic Weekdays

English	Icelandic	Translation
Sunday	Sunnudagur	sun-day
Monday	Mánudagur	moon-day
Tuesday	Thridjudagur	third-day
Wednesday	Midvikudagur	midweek-day
Thursday	Fimmtudagur	fifth-day
Friday	Föstudagur	fast-day
Saturday	Laugardagur	laundry-day

Traditionally in Iceland, mothers usually did the cooking. Today, however, both parents usually work, so they tend to share the household chores evenly. Time at home can be short, so it is not unusual for family members to help with shopping, dishes, laundry, and cleaning.

In the evenings, teenagers do homework and spend time watching television or texting their friends. Most homes have televisions, DVD or DVR players, and satellite dishes to pick

Skyr is one of the most common foods in Iceland.

Kartöflusalat

Potato salad, called *kartöflusalat* in Icelandic, accompanies many meals in Iceland. Have an adult help you with this recipe.

Ingredients

4 large potatoes, boiled, cooled, peeled, and cut in cubes

3 eggs, hard-boiled, cooled, and chopped

2 medium apples, peeled, cored, and cubed

6 small sweet pickles, chopped

¼ onion, finely chopped

¾ cup mayonnaise

¾ cup sour cream

1 tablespoon lemon juice

½ teaspoon curry powder

1 teaspoon salt

½ teaspoon pepper

Directions

Place the potatoes, chopped eggs, apple, pickles, and onion in a large bowl. In a smaller bowl, make the dressing by mixing the mayonnaise, sour cream, lemon juice, curry powder, salt, and pepper until smooth. Pour the dressing over the potatoes and other ingredients. Mix well. Cover and refrigerate for at least six hours. Enjoy!

up a wide range of television programs. There are sports channels, music video channels, public television, and channels that feature only real estate. Most Icelanders can also watch CNN, BBC, Sky News, and National Geographic, as well as many popular shows from the United States and a wide range of sports and news programs. The most popular locally produced show is *LazyTown*, which is aimed at preschool children.

What's to Eat?

In Iceland, the day generally starts with a simple breakfast. People often eat oatmeal or bread and butter. Adults enjoy a cup of coffee. Dairy products, including skyr, cottage cheese, whey, and yogurt, may also be eaten at breakfast.

Lunch may be packed from home or eaten out. Eating out offers a wide variety of foods. There are snack stands in most areas, and they serve hot dogs, grilled foods, hamburgers, dried fish, drinks, and chips. Quick meals can also be ordered at fried chicken restaurants, noodle shops, and cafés.

Icelanders do not tend to snack much, but they do like afternoon coffee break, with coffee and milk, cookies, cakes,

In the afternoon, Icelanders often gather for coffee and conversation.

and quick breads. There are cafés everywhere, and most Icelanders have open-faced sandwiches, bread and cheese, or skyr sometime between 2:30 and 4:00 p.m.

Dinner is eaten at 7:00 p.m., and usually consists of fish, lamb, or pork. Haddock, cod, salmon, herring, perch, and sole are served baked, grilled, salted, dried, or pickled. Local greenhouse fruits and vegetables, particularly apples, tomatoes, and cucumbers, are often part of the meal. There is usually another dish of skyr, but this time it has berries or sugar and cream.

Evening is a time when the family catches up on what has been happening with one another. The day ends late, with another round of coffee and pastries at about 9:00 p.m. for adults. Customs like these create bonds for families and friends, particularly through the dark, Icelandic winters.

Outdoor cafés are popular in Iceland during summer.

Timeline

Icelandic History

Possible sighting of Iceland by the Greek explorer Pytheas.	**ca. 330** BCE
Irish monks arrive in Iceland.	**ca. 600s– 700s** CE
The first settlers from Norway arrive in Iceland; Reykjavík is founded.	874
Althing, the first government meeting, is held.	930
Christianity is officially adopted in Iceland.	1000
Icelanders begin to compose in their native language.	ca.1100s
Norway begins ruling Iceland.	1262
Denmark, Sweden, and Norway, including Iceland, unite under a single monarch.	1397
A plague kills many Icelanders.	1402–1404
Denmark forbids Iceland from trading with other countries.	1602
Laki volcano erupts. It is the worst eruption in Icelandic history.	1783–1784

World History

ca. 2500 BCE	The Egyptians build the pyramids and the Sphinx in Giza.
ca. 563 BCE	The Buddha is born in India.
313 CE	The Roman emperor Constantine legalizes Christianity.
610	The Prophet Muhammad begins preaching a new religion called Islam.
1054	The Eastern (Orthodox) and Western (Roman Catholic) Churches break apart.
1095	The Crusades begin.
1215	King John seals the Magna Carta.
1300s	The Renaissance begins in Italy.
1347	The plague sweeps through Europe.
1453	Ottoman Turks capture Constantinople, conquering the Byzantine Empire.
1492	Columbus arrives in North America.
1500s	Reformers break away from the Catholic Church, and Protestantism is born.
1776	The U.S. Declaration of Independence is signed.
1789	The French Revolution begins.

Icelandic History

Iceland gets a new constitution.	**1874**
Iceland achieves home rule under Denmark.	**1904**
Iceland gains its independence, but the Danish monarch continues to be the chief of state.	**1918**
British troops occupy Iceland in World War II.	**1940**
Iceland ends its relationship with the Danish monarch and declares itself an independent republic.	**1944**
Surtsey, a new island, forms off Iceland's coast.	**1963**
Helgafell erupts, destroying many houses on Heimaey.	**1973**
Iceland extends its fishery limits to 200 miles (320 km), raising tensions with the United Kingdom.	**1975**
Vigdís Finnbogadóttir becomes the first woman elected president of a republic.	**1980**
Grímsvötn volcano erupts, creating problems for air traffic and sending ash as far as Finland.	**2004**
Iceland enters into a financial crisis.	**2008**
Iceland applies to join the European Union.	**2009**
Eyjafjallajökull volcano erupts with a massive ash cloud, disrupting air traffic in Europe for several days.	**2010**
Grímsvötn volcano erupts again.	**2011**

World History

1865	The American Civil War ends.
1879	The first practical lightbulb is invented.
1914	World War I begins.
1917	The Bolshevik Revolution brings communism to Russia.
1929	A worldwide economic depression begins.
1939	World War II begins.
1945	World War II ends.
1969	Humans land on the Moon.
1975	The Vietnam War ends.
1989	The Berlin Wall is torn down as communism crumbles in Eastern Europe.
1991	The Soviet Union breaks into separate states.
2001	Terrorists attack the World Trade Center in New York City and the Pentagon near Washington, D.C.
2004	A tsunami in the Indian Ocean destroys coastlines in Africa, India, and Southeast Asia.
2008	The United States elects its first African American president.

Fast Facts

Official name: Republic of Iceland

Capital: Reykjavík

Official language: Icelandic

Reykjavík

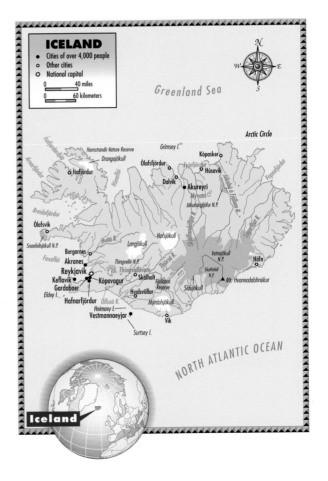

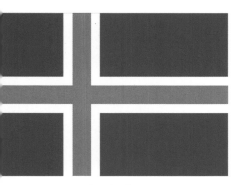

Icelandic flag

Mount Laki

Official religion: Lutheran Church of Iceland

National anthem: "Lofsöngur" ("Song of Praise")

Government: Constitutional republic

Chief of state: President

Head of government: Prime minister

Area of country: 39,769 square miles (103,001 sq km)

Highest elevation: Hvannadalshnúkur, 6,952 feet (2,119 m) above sea level

Lowest elevation: Sea level, along the coast

Longest river: Thjórsá, 143 miles (230 km)

Largest glacier: Vatnajökull, 3,100 square miles (8,100 sq km), and 3,300 feet (1,000 m) thick

Largest hot spring: Deildartunguhver, yields 50 gallons (190 L) of water per second

Largest lake: Thingvallavatn, 32 square miles (83 sq km)

Average high temperature: In Reykjavík, 35.4°F (1.9°C) in January; 55.9°F (13.3°C) in July

Average low temperature: In Reykjavík, 26.6°F (−3°C) in January; 46.9°F (8.3°C) in July

Lowest recorded temperature: −36.4°F (−38°C) at Grímsstadir in the northeast in 1918

Highest recorded temperature: 86.9°F (30.5°C) at the East Fjords in 1939

Strokkur Geyser

Currency

National population (2012 est.): 319,575

Population of major cities (2012 est.):

Reykjavík	136,354
Kópavogur	30,779
Hafnarfjördur	26,099
Akureyri	17,754
Gardabaer	10,909

Landmarks:
- ▶ *Blue Lagoon,* near Reykjavík
- ▶ *Dettifoss*, northeast Iceland
- ▶ *Hallgrímskirkja*, Reykjavík
- ▶ *Puffin colonies*, Vestmannaeyjar
- ▶ *Strokkur Geyser*, east of Reykjavík

Economy: Fishing and the industries it supports are major parts of the Icelandic economy. Food processing and metal manufacturing are important industries. Major crops include hay, cereal grains, and potatoes. Service industries make up a large part of the Icelandic economy, and tourism is particularly important. Iceland produces all of its electricity using geothermal and hydroelectric power.

Currency: Icelandic króna. In 2012, US$1.00 equaled 126 krónur, and 1 króna equaled US$0.01.

System of weights and measures: Metric system

Literacy rate (2006): 99%

College students

Björk

Common Icelandic words and phrases:

gódan dag	hello or good morning
góda kvöldid	good evening
Hvad heitir thú?	What is your name?
Ég heiti . . .	My name is . . .
Hvad segir thú?	How are you?
já	yes
nei	no
takk	thanks
bless	good-bye
Ég skil thad ekki.	I do not understand.

Prominent Icelanders:

Arnaldur Indrídason (1961–)
Novelist and journalist

Árni Magnússon (1663–1730)
Scholar who collected saga manuscripts

Björk (1965–)
Singer

Halldór Laxness (1902–1998)
Nobel Prize–winning author

Jóhannes Kjarval (1885–1972)
Painter

Snorri Sturluson (1179–1241)
Writer

Sveinn Björnsson (1881–1952)
First president of Iceland

Vigdís Finnbogadóttir (1930–)
First female president of Iceland

To Find Out More

Books

▶ Freedman, Russell. *Who Was First? Discovering the Americas*. New York: Clarion Books, 2007.

▶ Grant, Neil. *Eric the Red: True Lives*. New York: Oxford University Press, 2009.

▶ Prager, Ellen J., ed. *Volcano: Iceland's Inferno and Earth's Most Active Volcanoes*. Washington, DC: National Geographic, 2010.

▶ Van Rose, Susanna. *Volcano and Earthquake*. New York: DK Children, 2008.

Music

▶ Anna Gudny Gudmundsdóttir. *Svaviola II: Icelandic Music for Viola*. Reykjavík: Icelandic, 2008.

▶ Björk. *Biophilia*. New York: Nonesuch, 2011.

▶ Sigur Rós. *Valtari*. London: XL Recordings, 2012.

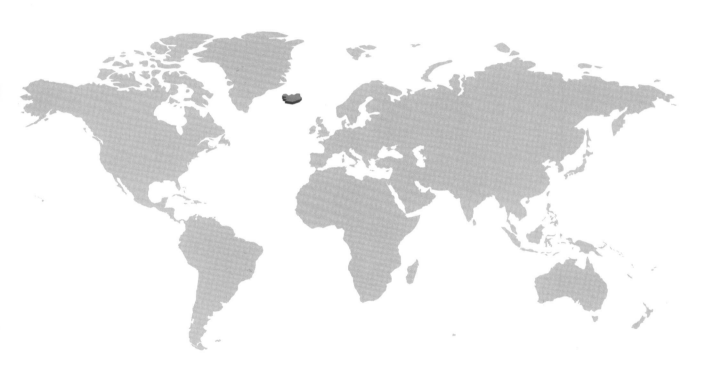

▶ Visit this Scholastic Web site for more information on Iceland:
www.factsfornow.scholastic.com
Enter the keyword Iceland

Index

Page numbers in *italics* indicate illustrations.

Meet the Author

Barbara Somervill has been writing children's nonfiction books for more than twenty years. She writes about countries, earth science, biographies, and social studies. This is her second book about Iceland, and although she has not had the opportunity to visit yet, it is on her "places I must visit" list. She says, "One of the joys of writing about a country is learning so much about the people, their customs, and the food they eat. I'm particularly interested in the fabulous sweaters that Icelanders wear. The patterns are unique and very beautiful."

Photo Credits